THE MONKS BEFORE CHRIST.

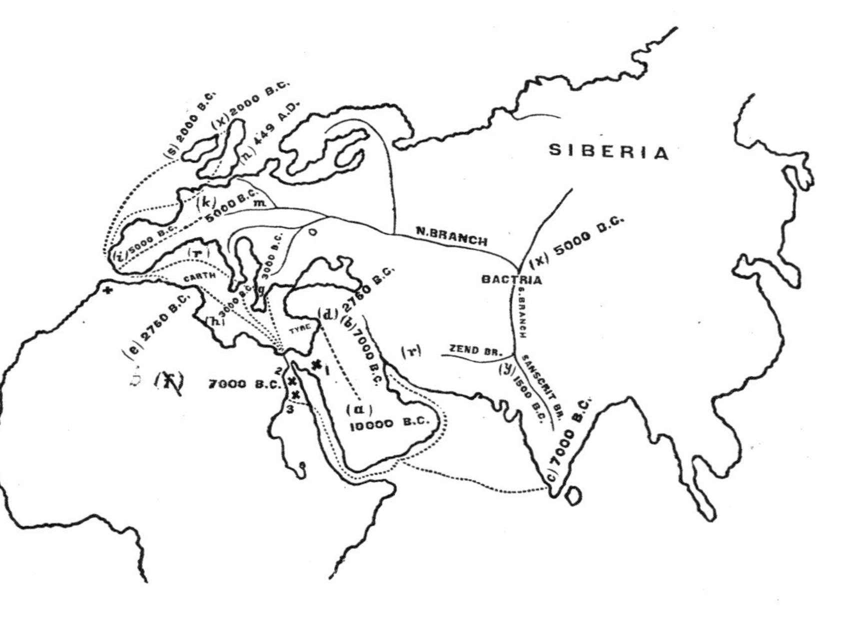

CHRONOLOGICAL CHART.—SEE PAGE 42.

THE MONKS BEFORE CHRIST:

Their Spirit and their History.

BY

JOHN EDGAR JOHNSON.

BOSTON:
A. WILLIAMS AND COMPANY.
1870.

TO

MRS. ELLEN C. JOHNSON,

A TRUE "SISTER OF CHARITY,"

WHO HAS NOT FOUND IT NECESSARY TO FORTIFY HERSELF AGAINST THE WORLD BY RETIRING FROM THE WORLD, BUT WHO WORKS IN AND THROUGH SOCIETY FOR THE WELFARE OF HER FELLOW MEN,

This Book is Affectionately Dedicated

BY HER FRIEND,

THE AUTHOR.

PREFACE.

IF there is a book in the world which accomplishes just what has been attempted in the following pages, I am ignorant of its existence. I was led to this study by a profound love and admiration for the monks; and I have felt at times the working of their spirit, and longed to be one of their number. If, then, it be thought that I have dealt with them too severely, let it be remembered that I am passing judgment upon myself.

It was my fortune to reside for several months at the Catholic University of Munich, in Bavaria, where I came in contact with members of the Order of Saint Benedict, and shall always remember that season as one of the most profitable in my religious experience. Had I been what the world would call a good Protestant, I did not then see, nor do I now, how I could have helped becoming a good Catholic; and this step taken, I would not have stopped short of its complete realization, — the monkish life.

At other times, I have discovered what seemed to me a higher standard of morality than that adopted by the monks; and a closer acquaintance with their mode of life, as it now exists in Europe, gave to the hopes which I once indulged a sad fall. Six months' observation in Southern France and Italy convinced me, that this institution was far from what I had thought to find it.

A visit to the monastery on Mount Cassim, founded by Saint Benedict in 429, did much to open my eyes to this fact. I was hospitably entertained; and the Brother who escorted me around the vast structure where I remained over night, was particularly kind; but when I mentioned to him my inclination to the monkish life, he declared that the time for making one's self a monk was now past, and then gave as a reason the fact that the monasteries had been deprived of their revenues, and their abbots of the titles which they used to bear.[1] I said

[1] The abbot of Mount Cassim was formerly the first baron in Italy.

to him that I thought them but poor disciples of the saint whose name they bore, if they allowed themselves to be cast down by circumstances such as these.

The next morning, I expressed considerable anxiety to my guide of the day before, on the score of my passport, which I had failed to have vised before leaving Naples for Rome. "Tell them that you have not been at Naples," he suggested. "But," I replied, "they will ask where I have been, and how I got from France into the Papal States." "Ah, I have it!" said he, "tell them you landed at Gaeta [a small port near Mount Cassim]; or, if you have to say Naples, tell them that the police there examined your passport, and said it was all right." "Great Heavens!" thought I, "and these are the men who had the exclusive manipulation of our Scriptures for several hundred years!"

I copy the following extract from my journal of that day: "On the whole, my visit to Mount Cassim, and conversation with the Brothers there, make me less confident than formerly that the monastic life belongs to the future." I visited, subsequently, several monasteries in Italy, and among others, the one upon the top of Mount Carvo, fourteen miles from Rome; but this feeling has gradually strengthened with me, from that time until now.

If, however, men and women can be prevailed upon to devote their lives to charitable works by holding up to them the inducement of a uniform or badge of office, make the offer by all means for the sake of an ulterior good. Just as we stimulate children with the promise of "rewards," and give a "banner" to the best class in Sunday school.

As for the historical chapters of this book, I must leave them to speak for themselves. Much of the research has been made in a field as yet quite unexplored; and the original documents have always been consulted when they were to be had.

If the reception of this volume should warrant the step, I purpose very soon to bring the study down to our own times. There are many histories of the different monastic orders in existence, but no available work in our language, as far as I am acquainted, which treats the subject of Christian monasticism in a concise and general manner. The plan of the future work would be nearly as follows: —

PERIOD FIRST. Early Christian Monasticism (Formative Period).

PERIOD SECOND. From Saint Benedict, the Lawgiver (429), until the founding of the first great order of Beggar Monks (1210).

PERIOD THIRD. History of the Beggar Monks until the Reformation (1517).

PERIOD FOURTH. From the Reformation until our time.

A chapter will be added on the Monastic Institutions of the United States of America.

The influence of the monks upon letters during the Middle and Dark Ages, the assistance rendered by them to the Popes in establishing the papal power, and the part played by them in the Reformation, are subjects to each of which a chapter would be devoted.

THE AUTHOR.

BRIGHTON, Mass.,
March, 1870.

CONTENTS.

PART FIRST.

THE SPIRIT OF THE MONKS.

CHAPTER I.

PAGE

The spirit of asceticism founded in human nature, and hence legitimate. Its grounds. Two kinds of asceticism. I. NEGATIVE. Three conclusions drawn from the conscious inability of man to attain to perfect goodness. The historical development of this principle, and its close connection with the belief in a personal devil. The three great manifestations of the monastic spirit: First, *Celibacy*. The high estimate in which this state is held in the Roman Catholic church, due to the system of Oriental dualism incorporated into her theology; testimony of the Catholic fathers in its favor: was it sanctioned by Jesus? Second, *Poverty*. How it expresses the monastic spirit; monkish garbs an evidence of vanity. Third, *Obedience*. Danger to the State from monkish vows; opposed to the spirit of Christianity. II. POSITIVE. Danger of self-contemplation; its selfishness; limitation; a moderate indulgence in self-examination salutary; man has two natures; the monk forgets this 3

PART SECOND.

HISTORY OF THE MONKS BEFORE CHRIST.

CHAPTER I.

Preparatory Remarks concerning the Origin and Spread of Ancient Civilizations.

PAGE

Importance of method in the study of history. Which is the oldest civilization? The Chinese. The Cushites. The Aryans. The emigrations of the last two families traced by means of a chart 37

CHAPTER II.

PAGAN MONKS.

Great antiquity of monasticism; as old as religion; Two sources of information, — monumental and biblical; The testimony of the former; the Sacred Books of the Ancients examined. *Chaldea.* The Nabatean Agriculture. Azada (about 4500 B.C.), the first great monk. *India.* The Vedas; The Law of Manu examined; Its monkish character; Gotama Buddha; Examination of the monkish code called the Winaya Pitaka. *Persia.* The Zend-Avesta. *China.* The Chou-King; Confucius a monk. *Greece.* The Order founded by Pythagoras; the Pagan Jesuits; Monasticism as it exists to-day in the East; Striking similarity between Hindoo monks and those of Christendom 51

CHAPTER III.

JEWISH MONKS.

PAGE

Elijah; John the Baptist. *The Essenes.* Sources from whence their history is drawn; *what* were the Essenes? extracts from Josephus showing them to be a monkish order; *who* were they? Attempts of modern critics to trace their origin. *The Therapeutæ.* Philo's account of them. A theory suggested to account for the origin of these two sects; the Essenes not mentioned in the New Testament; De Quincey identifies them with the early Christians; his theory confuted; attempts made to trace the origin of Christianity to Essenism; who made them; did Jesus Christ belong to this sect; the precepts and practices of each contrasted; this doctrine recently brought to life again; examination of the "Epistles of the Essenes;" the "Swooning" or "Resuscitation" theory, and how it accounts for the resurrection of Jesus; was Jesus Christ a monk? 109

PART FIRST.

THE SPIRIT OF THE MONKS.

THE SPIRIT OF THE MONKS.

CHAPTER I.[1]

The spirit of asceticism founded in human nature, and hence legitimate. Its grounds. Two kinds of asceticism. I. NEGATIVE. Three conclusions drawn from the conscious inability of man to attain to perfect goodness. The historical development of this principle, and its close connection with the belief in a personal devil. The three great manifestations of the monastic spirit: First, *Celibacy.* The high estimate in which this state is held in the Roman Catholic church, due to the system of Oriental dualism incorporated into her theology; testimony of the Catholic fathers in its favor: was it sanctioned by Jesus? Second, *Poverty.* How it expresses the monastic spirit; monkish garbs an evidence of vanity. Third, *Obedience.* Danger to the State from monkish vows; opposed to the spirit of Christianity. II. POSITIVE. Danger of self-contemplation; its selfishness; limitation; a moderate indulgence in self-examination salutary; man has two natures; the monk forgets this.

I WISH we knew who the first monk was; for then we should be able to solve that great biblico-ethnological question, "Who was the first man?" Monasticism is a phase of

[1] Richard Rothe, Theologische Ethik (Die Asketik); Jouffroy, Introduction to Ethics (System of Mysticism); Zöckler, Ueber Askese und deren Geschichte.

the religious nature of man. It is here that we are to seek its hidden meaning and its origin. "Every great error," says Dr. Clarke, "is a truth gone astray;" and we would infinitely prefer to be a monk, with all his fearful excesses, rather than be numbered among those who are totally strangers to the spirit which kindles and transports him. Men who get terribly in earnest about any thing in this world are impelled by genuine motives, and deserve mild and considerate treatment at our hands. The opinions and actions of our fellow-men are not to be held in detestation or laughed at, but — understood.[1]

There is one way to paint the monks, — as devils; another way, — as saints. In the latter case, relate the incidents of self-sacrifice and patient suffering with which their history abounds. In the former, dwell upon their cruel, immoral, and ambitious conduct; upon the crusades which they have preached against

[1] Hominum affectus et actiones nec detestari nec ridere, sed — intelligere. Spinoza, Ethic. lib. III. Proem.

heretics; upon the Massacre of Saint Bartholomew; upon their political intrigues in the Netherlands, in England, and in India; upon the Gunpowder Plot and the League. This is one mode of treating the subject: a better method is, to take both phases of their history into consideration, and then weigh one against the other.

Human nature is as varied as the physical surface of the globe. Thousands of persons have never been in China; and thousands more are strangers to the impulse which moves the monk. Four fifths of human nature are ignorant of the other fifth. Hence it would be no more unreasonable for a Protestant American to dispute with an inhabitant of the Celestial Empire about his native country, than for the former to engage in a controversy with a monk as to whether the monastic life is a natural want of any portion of mankind. For some men it may be a very legitimate desire; but between them and the rest of the world, there flows a broad ocean under which it is possible to lay down an electric cable, but over which there exists, for thousands at least, no means of transportation.

There are as many varieties of human nature as there are of Holland tulips. But now and then some person succeeds in cultivating a tulip, until no one knows, any longer, what it is. It cannot be recognized as a tulip. Just so, by dwelling upon, stimulating, and drawing out to an inordinate extent a particular phase of human nature, — a propensity of the soul, — it is possible to produce a new variety of the *genus homo*, — a monk.

Now and then, too, a Chinaman may be found who not only maintains the real existence of his native country, but insists that it is the only one worth living in. The monks sometimes imagine that they have found the "Celestial Empire."

A phase of religion is the universal longing after perfect godliness: *monasticism springs from man's inability to attain to it.* Catholicism aims at the accomplishment of this end by means of "good works," and, if its doctrine were legitimately carried out, would finish by annihilating the human race. The child that clutches at the sun, exhausts itself in a vain effort. No man ever felt that he deserved much at the hands of the Almighty; and the monks of the Thebaid — who passed day and night in almost uninterrupted fasting, tears, and lacerations of the body — dared only hope that their "good works" might atone, at most, for the evil which they constantly fell into. Between these two millstones, — the impossibility of human perfection, and the attempt to attain to it, — mankind had soon been ground to powder.

Protestantism, terrified at the fearful excesses of asceticism, maintained that godliness was entirely independent of works, and could be attained by faith alone. This doctrine, when considered in the abstract, appears to justify the charge of licentiousness which has frequently been brought against it, and to discourage the exercise of practical virtue. A medium course affords the only escape from such extreme theories.

It is difficult to believe that God would ever demand perfection at the hands of a being whom he has created imperfect; that he would take special care that man might not contain within him the *possibility* of perfect goodness in this life, and then punish him for not attaining to it. "Be ye, therefore, perfect as your Father which is in heaven is perfect," should not be literally interpreted, as may be shown by many other texts in the Scriptures. This injunction places before us a high aim, *towards* which man should ever struggle, but *to* which it is neither expected nor required that he attain. Such is the answer to Protestantism.

Against the Catholics it should be maintained, that there are not two eternal principles in the universe, but one; that the body does not belong to the devil, but to God, and is his work; that virtue is active, and that the passions are given to us for our good, and should be controlled, not annihilated. "It is much easier to extinguish our first desire, than it is to regulate and satisfy those that follow it."[1]

Asceticism, we have said, rests upon the longing after perfect godliness; and it finds expression in two ways:

I. Negative. It revenges itself upon the body, which drags the soul down, and prevents the accomplishment of its desire. It vents its spite upon the passions, — those sentinels appointed by the Almighty, whose purpose it is to create subordinate souls and not co-ordinate ones.

II. Positive. The soul sinks itself in contemplation of the supreme good.

The monk hated the world as the work of the devil, and his body as the means by which he was brought in contact with it. At different times he has pursued two opposite courses with regard to the treatment of his body. He began by trying to wear it out, but finally concluded to let it rust out. The monks in Egypt

[1] Rochefoucauld.

were agriculturists; and Saint Benedict, in the sixth century, prescribed seven hours' manual labor every day. Usually, however, monasticism has evinced a profound contempt for all action, — intellectual, physical, and sexual.

We have alluded to the conscious inability of man to attain to that perfect good which he longs after. Now there are three conclusions which may be drawn from that fact, and we mention them in their historic order: —

1st. There are two creating principles in the universe, a good and a bad; to the former we owe the living soul of man, and to the latter the material world and our bodies. This doctrine was known to the early Christian church under the name of Manicheism, but is, in its original form, as old as man himself.

2d. As the belief in one God gradually supplanted polytheism, it became necessary to account for this discrepancy between man's desire and his power of accomplishment; and the doctrine of "the fall of man" was then evolved.

3d. As more just ideas of the character of God came to prevail, men revolted, as from blasphemy, against the supposition that the Almighty would require impossibilities from any of his creatures. The object of life has come to be regarded as the formation of character. Virtue is active, and man was already too noble for paradise when he was driven forth from it. "If he ever fell," says Dr. Bellows, "he certainly *fell up*, for he has been growing nobler and better ever since." Evil is that divine collodion which (in the hand of the great Artist) serves to bring out and develop the hidden features in the human soul.

Thus the doctrine of mysticism follows invariably either from the doctrine of Manicheism, or that of "the fall of man;" and it is only by accepting the last of these conclusions enumerated above that we are able to refute it.

Let us follow the principle, however, in its historic development. The belief in a personal devil[1] is probably as old as the belief in a personal God. The idea of unseen spirits owed its origin, in the minds of the first men, to the death of some of their fellow-creatures. They recognized in nature certain phenomena which they felt obliged to attribute to an intelligent cause. All propitious occurrences were looked upon as the work of good spirits; all inimical events were traced back to the agency of bad ones. When the sun shone, the crops grew, or success crowned their efforts in the chase or upon the war-path, that was the work of God; but when the lightning struck their cabins, or the torrent swept away their harvests, that was the work of the devil. And, henceforth, he became essential to the existence and development of asceticism. Evoked by the belief in Satan, the monastic life began to fall into disrepute so soon as the world began to question his existence; and their destinies have been so closely interlaced that

[1] Dr. Schenkel says there never was a belief in a personal devil, — only a superstition.

the biography of the former would be the history of the latter. Quite recently an attempt has been made to resuscitate the devil. We have been told that "the moral apathy of our time is the result of disbelief in a personal devil," and that "the devil forms a background for the better display of God's attributes."[1] It remains to be seen what success will crown this effort at resuscitation. One thing, however, is certain, that asceticism, which could not survive the decease of the devil, will spring into new life, the moment he is revived again.

Under the head of negative asceticism may properly be considered the three great vows which have characterized monastic institutions in all time. These are celibacy, poverty, obedience.

Celibacy. The monk, it has been said, re-

[1] Martensen. Das Bewusstsein von dem dämonischen Reiche und dem Fürsten desselben ist der dunkle, nächtliche Hintergrund für das christliche Bewusstsein, und die Furcht von dem Teufel und das tiefe Grauen vor der dämonischen Gemeinschaft der dunkle Grund für die christliche Gottesfurcht.

garded his body as the work of the devil; and hence he shrank with horror from the satisfaction of its wants. Of course, all sexual indulgence was a mortal sin; and the state of celibacy was exalted far above that of marriage. "The state of Christian celibacy," says a Catholic writer,[1] "is so eminent and so perfect, that neither the Pagan philosophers have formed any idea of it, nor was it known to the Ancient Law; while even the New Law has recommended rather than commanded it. Saint John Chrysostom, who knew so well the price and merit of it, did not fear to elevate this state above that of marriage, and even maintained its equality with the condition of the angels. 'If marriage,' said he, 'is not for the angels, it is not for the virgins.' Thus it is that Saint Cyprian has called them 'the beauty and ornament of spiritual grace, that divine image which corresponds to the holiness of our Lord Jesus Christ.'"

[1] M. Jean Baptiste Thiers, Traité de la Clôture des Religieuses, Paris, 1681.

The same author further remarks, that "virginity is something so delicate and so fragile, that the least injury which it may receive is capable of tarnishing its *éclat* and the lustre which accompanies it." "It is extremely important," continues he, "for Christian virgins, who wish to make sure the grace of their divine vocation and render themselves worthy of the love and caresses of their Lord Jesus Christ, in the character of his spouses, that they fortify themselves outside of the world against the world, and that they place themselves out of the reach of all the criminal temptations which may possibly come from abroad."

Saint Ambrose says, that "the virgins, by the observance of their vows, attain to the general resurrection by enjoying in advance, in this world, the glorious advantages which even the elect enjoy only after the day of universal judgment."

Saint Francis de Salès has also lauded the state of celibacy (see epistle to an Abbess, No 50).

Such is the doctrine of the Catholic Church to-day; and it rests wholly upon the system of Oriental dualism which has been embodied in her theology. She places celibacy higher than marriage, and yet permits no divorce, the inconsistency of which will be seen at once. Why insist so tenaciously upon the observance of an institution of such subordinate value? There are two passages of Scripture which would seem to justify her position; viz., Matt. xxii. 30, where Christ declares that in heaven they "neither marry nor are given in marriage;" and also 1 Cor. vii. 7, where the apostle Paul expresses the wish that all men might be as he was,—that is, single. We reply to any argument which may be based upon the first text as follows: There may be things eminently proper and necessary in this world which would be decidedly out of place and unnecessary in the next one. Among these may be reckoned the propagation of our species, without which Christianity itself must soon cease to exist. With regard to the second text we remark,—1st, Saint Paul was in the minority among the apostles in this respect. 2dly, He had no idea of extolling celibacy, in itself, above marriage, but only preferred it for his followers on account of the troubled state of the times, the persecution to which they were subject, and the supposed proximity of the second coming of Christ. His view of the sanctity of marriage in itself, may be inferred from the fact that he has compared it to the relation which exists between Christ and his church.

This is one of the most pernicious doctrines of the Catholic church, but is a legitimate consequence of the character which she assigns to virtue; viz., freedom from every thing which pertains to the body, as the work of Satan. God has given us our passions for a good purpose. Virtue is active: it is the result of a temptation overcome, or the reward of the moderate exercise of our powers. The monk finds it much easier to bolt the door upon his passions, than he does to regulate and control them. Virtue is a state of the heart; and the purest souls in heaven, those close around the throne of God, are mothers. Swedenborg said, that, although the virgins he saw in heaven were beautiful, the wives were incomparably more beautiful, and went on increasing in beauty evermore.

"'So celibacy is the highest state?' And why? 'Because it is the safest and the easiest road to heaven.' A pretty reason! I should have thought that was a sign of a lower state, and not a higher. Noble spirits show their nobleness by daring the most difficult paths. And even if marriage were but one weed-field of temptation,—as these miserable pedants say, who have never tried it or misused it to their own shame,—it would be a greater deed to conquer its temptations than to fly from them in cowardly longings after ease and safety."[1] "It is as unreasonable," says Dr. Johnson, "for a man to go into a Carthusian convent for fear of being immoral,

[1] Charles Kingsley.

as for a man to cut off his hands for fear he should steal."[1]

Poverty. In India, the Fakirs go stark naked. In Paris, the Lazarists *borrow* the clothing which they wear. Money is the means which we employ to satisfy our material wants. By thrusting it contemptuously from us, we cast a reproach upon the values which it represents. Hence voluntary poverty was one of the first expressions of the monastic spirit. It has always been regarded as the sign of a special and extraordinary sanctity. "Freedom from every lien which binds us to the body" was the watchword of the monk; and he found it much easier to renounce wealth altogether, than to employ it judiciously and generously. The most that can be said against this practice is, that it does violence to nature. God seems to have planted in every human breast the desire to provide for the future. Competency is a duty: only the morally lazy can desire pov-

[1] Boswell's Life of Johnson.

erty. He who does not wish to be rich cannot love his fellow-men. If the monk would employ himself actively, make the best of all his powers, apply the result of his labors to the amelioration of the lot of his neighbor, devoutly trust in God for the future, and rely upon Him who sends the "rainy days" to supply him with a shelter, his course would be a most commendable one. But when he resolves neither to have nor earn money, and sinks his soul in idle contemplation of the Supreme Being, he makes a great mistake. It is worthy of notice that a great majority of the monks have never been severely tempted with regard to worldly possessions; and some one has remarked, that people who affect to despise wealth wish to revenge themselves against the injustice of fortune by manifesting a contempt for that of which they are deprived. "It is a secret means of insuring one's self against the degradation of poverty. It is a roundabout way of reaching that consideration to which we are unable to attain by means of riches."

Others are willing to sacrifice great worldly possessions for an odor of distinguished sanctity in this life, or hoping to drive a good bargain with the future one. "Some, without any doubt," says a Catholic writer, "without any inclination for solitude, have consecrated themselves to the Lord out of pure pride." The Council of Orleans found it necessary to decree "that no monk should abandon, out of ambition or pride, the monastery to which he belongs, for the purpose of constructing a cell by himself."

The monk has always wished to distinguish himself by a particular garb; and the more striking it was, the better he seemed to like it. It is doubtful if any monastic order could long exist without some such outward badge of holiness. Even the "Sisters of Charity," in some respects a most admirable organization, betray a weakness in this direction. Look at their deep collars, white bonnets, and heavy cross, and then judge how much

[1] Massillon.

vanity may possibly have to do with their piety. Why are not people satisfied to do good in an unostentatious manner? Why can they not practise the heavenly virtues, and at the same time discharge their daily duties? We are satisfied that self-love lies at the bottom of all such institutions; granted, a high order of self-love. The first impulse of a man, spiritually moved, may be to connect himself with a monastic order; but, as his religious experience deepens, he sees the refined selfishness of such a course, and realizes that his heaviest cross is to be sought in the world, and in bearing with the infirmities of his fellow-men. How the cheap virtue of a Sister of Charity sinks into insignificance when compared with the heroism of the thousands of pure-minded women who remain in society and employ themselves — to take a single instance — in the education of youth! People like to advertise their goodness; they wish to belong to a "good Society"— one that makes a business of being good. A flowing gown, or a white linen bonnet and collar, make it so easy to love God and be just. It is not difficult to act nobly when one is all alone. How often we make resolutions which we fail to keep! The effort, the struggle which we make,—that is virtue: resolution has no positive worth. Now this difference between resolving and doing is just the difference between passive and active virtue,—between doing good with your every-day clothes on, and doing good with your distinctively pious habiliments on; between going into a monastery, and discharging your duties among your fellow-men.

But, at another time, perhaps, we may show how the monks have always repudiated their vows of poverty whenever the munificence of their superstitious patrons has rendered it profitable, and to what contemptible chicanery and artifice they have resorted, in order to reconcile their personal poverty with the scandalous opulence of the monasteries to which they belonged.

Obedience. Obedience was made by Saint Benedict (529) the first of monkish virtues. Saint Bernard (1113) said to the monks of his order, "If an angel from heaven should command me to do any thing contrary to my rule, I would refuse an obedience which would render me a transgressor of my own vows." Ignatius Loyola (1532) enjoined obedience to superiors, even to the commission of mortal sins. Hence the Jesuits have often perjured themselves; they have lied and calumniated whenever it promised to advance the interest of their order. The danger of such an institution, to the state, may easily be imagined. To this principle, boldly pushed to the end, the Jesuits may possibly owe their expulsion from every European country. A Roman citizen once said, "If my brother should order me to burn the capitol, I would burn it." It is needless to say that the physical liberty of that Roman was forthwith restrained. A French writer, already cited,[1] has

[1] M. Jean Baptiste Thiers.

entered into a lengthy discussion of the causes which justify a monk or nun in breaking their claustral vows. He devotes one chapter of his book to the consideration of the subject, "Whether the 'Religieuses' are justified in leaving their convent in case of a great fire which threatens to destroy the building." Several church fathers are quoted to support the affirmative of this question. Many instances are also adduced which would seem to justify it.

Another chapter considers, whether an unhealthy climate, or danger of an inundation, is cause sufficient for such abandonment; and the author shows conclusively that bad air is *not* a sufficient justification for such a step, inasmuch as, in many cases, the sites of these cloisters have been chosen expressly on this account. (See in particular St. Bernard, Epistle 321, and, better still, Epistle 384). "Freshets" are decided to be inadequate; but "inundations" have several fathers and one or two popes on their side.

Still another chapter considers, whether monks and nuns are justified in leaving their retreats when the walls are threatened with overthrow; and here the writer shows conclusively again that several councils, and a large number of popes and prelates, have decided this to be sufficient cause for taking such a step. Finally, the question is asked whether famine justifies such abandonment; and the answer is a negative one.

"To be dead to myself, to have no longer a will of my own, no will, no temper, no opinions,"[1] such is the Catholic doctrine of obedience. Let us see how it agrees with that of the New Testament. If the Divine Master has taught obedience to kings and princes, where has he prescribed that servile subordination which robs a man of all independence, all dignity, all personality? In what passage of the Sacred Book is it taught that a creature made in the image of God ought to obey like a corpse, *perinde ac cadaver*.[2] Such a rule

[1] Bourdaloue, Retraite Spirituelle.
[2] Rule of the Jesuits.

of life may be found in the Code of Brahminism; but the New Testament speaks, on the contrary, of the glorious liberty of the children of God, (Rom. viii. 2), and recommends us to rest firm in the liberty to which Christ has called us (Gal. v. 1). Christian perfection is the sister of progress and liberty.

Thus far we have dwelt upon the first or negative form of asceticism: let us now proceed to consider the second or active expression of the monastic spirit. The monk sinks himself in contemplation of the perfect good. To be plunged in God, and grow with him like a flame, — that is the mystic's purpose. He loses sight of the distinction which must always exist between self-consciousness and God-consciousness. The relation which exists between these two will ever remain a mystery. One thing, however, is certain, — man's individuality should never be lost sight of. Mysticism (from μύω, to see with closed eyes) forgets tha' fact; it arises from an imperfect, that is to say, a one-sided, development of consciousness. Self-contemplation plunges man into the abyss of self-deification and self-satisfaction. Self-examination, when carried to excess, is a species of vanity. We flatter ourselves when we think to discover a great many faults and errors in our own hearts. Hence the pernicious character of such "spiritual exercises" as those prescribed by the Jesuits. Do not probe your motives too deeply. Some one has remarked that it is as injudicious and unprofitable as pulling up a plant for the purpose of examining its roots. If you search your heart too closely, the chances are that you will conclude in the end that there is no such thing as virtue; and in this event there are two alternatives, — turn fatalist or monk. You will abandon yourself to sensuality and utter godlessness, adopting the atheist's motto, "Let us live while we live, for to-morrow we die;" or you will be drawn into ascetic practices of the most hopeless kind. Do not brood over the secret springs of action; forget yourself, if it be possible.

Forget, in your zeal for others, that you have a soul of your own to save. Know that there is but one crime in the world, — to remember yourself; and there is but one virtue, — to forget yourself.

All that has been said upon this subject should be taken with its proper limitations. The New Testament recommends self-examination (Matt. vii. 3 and 1 Cor. xi. 31); not as an *end*, however, but only as a *means*. It should prepare us for the better performance of our duties towards our fellow-men. For "if we would judge ourselves, we should not be judged." Let an hour, now and then, be set aside for meditation and self-examination. Never enter upon any great work without having devoted a short time to solitude. "One hour of secret meditation and silent prayer," says a Persian poet, "is of more worth than seventy thousand years of outward worship." This would be an excellent practice for the clergyman. Let him do it *before* preparing his sermon rather than *afterwards;* otherwise honesty may oftentimes compel him to sacrifice the results of a week's labor. Christ went into the wilderness and fasted forty days, just before entering upon his ministry. The world has never produced a great man, nor a noble, virtuous woman, who was not educated to some extent by solitude. In those quiet moments, God ordained them for their high and noble office. But society is not to be abandoned: it is man's native element. "Man is more social than any bee." Solitude is a bath which cleanses us from the impurities of active life, and refreshes and invigorates us for a new effort. "Whosoever delights altogether in solitude is either a wild beast or a God" (Aristotle). Contemplation makes us acquainted with ourselves. By this means we fix our *human vocation* in the eye; but never lose sight of its mediate character. "Protracted solitude," says De Wette, "brings with it emptiness of spirit, for the spirit can enrich itself only in active life." To fast is good. Fast; but do it because it is quite impossible to think or pray upon a full stomach: one falls asleep. The genuine observation of a day of national fasting and prayer would be productive of much good. But never run away from the world: it is an act of moral cowardice. The monk seeks extravagant methods of atonement: why not try that most severe of all, — the practice of virtue under severe temptation? Why not remain in society and help purify it? If you are to crucify the flesh, let the world be your cross, and there is none like it, — and do not rob the world of *its* cross by taking yourself out of it. If God's providence is manifested in any one thing more than another, it is in the gradual uplifting of his people, in the civilization and moral education of society. If you abandon his grand experiment in this life, he will abandon your soul in the life which is to come. "You deserted from my standard there below: I have pensions laid up only for those who bravely met the foe, fought their way through the temptations of life, and rose victorious above them all. Devote yourself to any form of self-culture that you choose; but know that complete forgetfulness of self, and devotion to the good of others, is the only virtue which I recognize in man." The remoteness from God, implied by words such as these, is much more to be feared than the most terrible conception of a material hell.

Man is a creature of two worlds, — the material and the spiritual. He belongs to both of them. We are citizens as well as pilgrims, — citizens of this world, pilgrims of the next. We are born of the earth, and should not live outside of the world, but in it. We ought not to abstain from the exercise of our passions: it is our duty to work through them. The monk attempts to steal *around* the world, and therefore is cowardly. We must force our way *through* in order to win the hero's crown. The ruined cloisters of Europe remind one that moral cowardice was once nourished and applauded.

"But men who abandon themselves to a

contemplative life do no harm, and think only on God: have they no merit in his eyes? No; for if they do no harm, neither do they perform any good, and hence they are useless: moreover, not to do good is already to do evil. God wishes man to think of him, but not of him alone, since he has given man duties to perform towards his fellow-men. He who consumes himself in meditation and prayer has no merit in the sight of God, since his life is wholly personal and useless to humanity; and *God will demand account of him for the good which he has* NOT *done.*"[1]

[1] Allan Kardec, Le livre des Esprits.

NOTE. — This chapter appeared in the form of an article in the Universalist Quarterly for Jan. 1870.

PART SECOND.

HISTORY OF THE MONKS BEFORE CHRIST.

ANCIENT CIVILIZATIONS.

CHAPTER I.

PREPARATORY REMARKS CONCERNING THE ORIGIN AND SPREAD OF ANCIENT CIVILIZATIONS.[1]

Importance of method in the study of history. Which is the oldest civilization? The Chinese. The Cushites. The Aryans. The emigrations of the last two families traced by means of a chart.

TRUE to the principle laid down at the commencement of the last chapter, I begin the search after the first development of the monastic spirit by a few inquiries into the origin of the human race. For society was no sooner formed than men began to withdraw themselves from it: they sought

[1] Max Müller, Essays on the Science of Religion. John D. Baldwin, A.M., Pre-Historic Nations. New York: Harper & Brothers. 1869.

P. F. Stuhr. Allgemeine Geschichte der Religionsformen der heidnischen Völker. (das Urvolk.)

the solitude, the wilderness, the desert. In exploring this field it is of the utmost importance that we proceed methodically. Unless we adopt some general plan in the study of history, we labor almost in vain. That which is read to-day, for want of arrangement or association, is forgotten to-morrow. Goethe says, "Contents without method leads to straggling thought; method without contents to empty theorizing; matter without form to a burdensome knowledge; form without matter to a vain delusion."[1] Early in life one is possessed by the desire to trace nationalities back to some common origin, — to arrange, to classify, and to compare all the peoples of which we have any account. We seek to derive one from the other, to construct a chronological tree or river; and, in the attempt to realize our idea, we cover sheets of paper with all sorts of historical plans. In a short

[1] Gehalt ohne Methode führt zur Schwärmerei, Methode ohne Gehalt zum leeren Klügeln, Stoff ohne Form zum beschwerlichen Wissen, Form ohne Stoff zu einem hohlen Wähnen.

time we become involved in the most inextricable confusion; and our last diagram reminds one of an Egyptian or Cretan labyrinth. At this stage in our studies we take up, perhaps, some work like "Nott and Glidden on the Types of Mankind," and here we learn, — alas, for our plan! — that "the human race was scattered broadcast over the face of the earth like vegetables and animals." This puts an end, for the time being, to all of our chronological aspirations.

A more judicious selection of authors, however, soon resuscitates the old opinion and along with it our former purpose. By the aid of comparative philology, we are soon able to trace all existing races back to three or four original sources; while the same great elements of human nature which characterize them all, encourage us to believe that somewhere in the hoary past the ancestors of the billion souls which now inhabit the earth have slept together in one common cradle, and spoken the same tongue.

In any historical map or chart which may be constructed, that stream which is intended to represent the Chinese Empire will always flow uninterruptedly from top to bottom without tributaries or outlets — if we make two exceptions.

About 1259 the Mongols overran China, but were expelled in the following century. Nearly two hundred years later, the Manchoo Tartars conquered the country, and have remained its masters ever since.

The Chinese is the only specimen of a primitive language now in existence, and is monosyllabic in its form. It has a written literature which claims to be nineteen centuries older than the Christian era. China has never been an aggressive power; and, until quite recently, she has had a wonderfully simple "Foreign Policy." As a natural consequence, she has exerted little or no civilizing influence upon the nations by which she is surrounded.

Two great waves of civilization have swept

over the world in past times; and to these we propose to confine our attention. The earlier proceeded from the south and spread east and west; the later had its starting-point in the north and propagated itself west and south. The authors of the first of these movements were the Cushites of Southern Arabia, the ancient Ethiopia of the Greeks and Romans. The latter was carried on by the Aryan race, that inhabited, originally, the northern portion of Asia or Southern Siberia, which at that time must have had a mild and favorable climate.[1] One of these migrations took place almost entirely by land; while the other was altogether naval in its character.

Baldwin is undoubtedly right in maintaining that the Cushites preceded the Aryans by

[1] Within a few years, several mastodon or elephants have been found imbedded in the ice of Southern Siberia, and one was in such a state of preservation that its flesh was immediately devoured by the dogs which accompanied the exploring party. This shows quite conclusively that the climate of Northern Asia was once much milder than at the present time. Perhaps the migration of the Aryan race was brought about by some great change which the temperature subsequently underwent.

many centuries in India, Persia, Greece, Italy, and Spain. Let us, then, attempt to indicate the movements of these two streams of civilization.

If the reader will turn to the chart facing title-page, and trace with a pencil the route pursued by each of these two great families in its migration, it will help him to understand the whole subject of this chapter. The letters in the text refer to corresponding letters on the chart.

Unmistakable evidences point to the extreme antiquity of the Cushite race in Arabia. Recent developments, which have been gained from the ruins of this country, will justify us in supposing that Southern Arabia was in a state of civilization not later than 10,000 B.C. (*a*).[1] The Cushites were a nation of navigators, and carried on their colonization by means

[1] By experiments made at the statue of Rameses in Egypt, Bunsen has shown quite conclusively that the Nile valley was peopled by a civilized race more than 11,000 years B.C. Cushite civilization must be many centuries older than that of Egypt.

of their ships. Cushite civilization extended to the valleys of the Nile and Euphrates not later than 7000 B.C. (*b*), and to India very soon afterwards (*c*). Of this there can now be little doubt. The language of the inscriptions found in these countries bears a marked resemblance to that which has been discovered in Southern Arabia. Professor Rawlinson, in his work on Herodotus, uses the following words, "Recent linguistic discovery tends to show that a Cushite or Ethiopian race did, in the earliest times, extend itself along the shores of the Southern Ocean from Abyssinia to India. The whole peninsula of India was peopled by a race of this character before the influx of the Aryans; it extended along the sea-coast through the modern Beloochistan and Kerman; the cities on the northern shores of the Persian Gulf are shown by the brick inscriptions found in its ruins to have belonged to this race." These adventurous navigators found civilization among all the people whom they visited, but from whence it came is more than can now be ascertained. Bunsen says, the origin of man antedates the Christian Era, more than 20,000 years;[1] and, if so, civilization must be equally as old, for there is reason to believe that this was the original state of mankind. There is no instance on record where a savage people have risen to civilization without outside assistance, although the reverse may sometimes have been true.

Herodotus says the Phœnicians founded Tyre 2760 B.C. (*d*), and they probably went to Carthage about the same time (*e*). Now we know that these Phœnicians were a part of the old Cushite race which forced its way

[1] The question may arise, "How far may the antiquity of man *possibly* be carried back?" Geologists have found no human remains in any period prior to that which is now forming. To this belong the alluvial deposits of the Mississippi delta, and perhaps the lower half of the peninsula of Florida. The former is computed to have been in progress at least 100,000 years; while the latter is said by Agassiz to have occupied more than 130,000 years in its formation. Consequently, any theory which does not carry the origin of the human race further back than about 100,000 years, *if well established by scientific investigation*, ought not to challenge our credulity. But thus far, the verdict of cool science, as opposed to such theories, is — Not proven.

northward into Canaan, and finally settled upon the coast of the Mediterranean Sea (*f*).

The Greeks, even before Herodotus, were accustomed to trace their civilization to Egypt; and this was perhaps the first attempt ever made towards the discovery of a primitive race. Thus it will be seen that "Pre-Historic Times" was a problem which agitated the world at a very early date.

The superiority, in point of antiquity, of Chaldean over Egyptian civilization, was soon made evident; while recent investigation has shown quite conclusively that Arabia was the cradle of them both. Cushite civilization was carried to Greece from Egypt 3000 B.C. (*g*), and to Italy at nearly the same time (*h*). It had passed from North Africa over into Spain not later than 5000 B.C. (*i*), from whence it found its way soon after into France (*k*). The rock-cut temples of India, Phœnicia, Egypt, Greece, and Italy, all resemble those found in Arabia and are of immense antiquity.

Having thus briefly pointed out the time

and manner in which Cushite civilization spread over a large part of Europe, Southwestern Asia, and Northern Africa, we will now attempt to indicate the course pursued by the Aryan race in its migrations. (See again frontispiece).

"Before the beginning of traditional history, the Aryan tribes lived north of the Himalaya mountains with the ancestors of the Greeks, Italians, Germans, Celts, and Sclavonians" (Max Müller).

We shall be justified in placing that period at 5000 B.C. (*x*). The whole family dwelt, as yet, under one roof; and the division may not have taken place until a long time after the date above mentioned. The race divided into two branches, which have been called the north and south branches. The former proceeded in a north-westerly direction, and conquered Europe; the latter passed southward, and spread out over India, Persia, and Northern Arabia. The Hindoos, although the oldest branch, were probably the last to leave the parental roof, and the Vedas must have been written in Upper India several centuries after their arrival, say 1500 B.C. (*y*).

Long before this, however, a violent schism had taken place between the Brahmins and the followers of Zoroaster,—the first great Aryan reformer, the Martin Luther of Brahminism, he who did not hesitate to brand the priests of those times as Antichrist, if we may speak thus, and turned many of their gods into his devils. But separation did not take place until after they had dwelt together for some time in Hindostan, where those who have since been known as Magians or Fire-Worshippers, at last bade adieu to India and passed over into Persia.

Their sacred writings, the Zend-Avesta, were already in existence 400 B.C. (*v*); for Alexander is said to have destroyed the books of the Zoroastrians.

The Persian records, it should be borne in mind, go far back of Persia. Long before she appeared as a nation, Bactria—the probable scene of Zoroaster's life — was the capital of an Aryan kingdom where the Zend and Sanscrit branches lived together and used a common language. The latter dwelt many centuries in Upper India previous to the completion of the Vedas, as some of the older portions were written 2400 B.C.; while the Avesta may have been preserved as oral tradition long after the Zoroastrians arrived in Persia. The people whom the Aryans found in Southern Asia, it should not be forgotten, were all enjoying a high degree of civilization; and Southern India and Persia held out for a long time against Aryan invasion and amalgamation. The Vedas show that these people had large cities and cultivated the arts; and it is not difficult to identify them with the old Cushite race, whose migrations we have already traced.

The migration of the northern branch of the Aryan family cannot be so precisely indicated. Although the first to set out, they did not reach Germany until about the beginning of our era (*m*); and from thence they passed into England where they date from the Saxon conquest, 449 A.D. (*n*). Here they had been preceded, however, by the Celts, who were a race of mixed origin as will be explained further on. In Greece and Italy they arrived at a very early date (*o*); and the mythologies of those countries embody, without doubt, something of the dimly remembered history of their wanderings. In the latter country, they were known by the name of Pelasgians. The Etruscans, a Cushite race without doubt, had preceded them, however, as we have already pointed out.

If we are to judge from the analogy of language, we conclude that the Aryans, who first came to Spain, were Italians (*r*). Here a blending took place between them and the old Cushite race, from whence sprang the Celts, a people who soon passed northward to the shores of Ireland,[1] where they arrived

[1] Prior to this the Formorians had come to Ireland from Africa, sometime during the Age of Bronze, or about 3000 B.C.

many centuries before the beginning of our era, say about 2000 B.C. (*s*), and soon crossed over into Scotland (*t*). About this time, an emigration of the Celts took place from Spain to France; and from there they passed across the channel into England and Wales.

In the foregoing brief summary of the origin and progress of ancient Cushite and Aryan civilization, it is not possible to attain to any considerable degree of accuracy in the matter of dates; but we may feel quite certain that the stream flowed much in the same manner and direction as that which has been indicated.

Having now cleared the ground of a vast amount of historical rubbish, and systematized our knowledge somewhat, we may venture to approach more nearly the real subject which we have at heart.

CHAPTER II.[1]

PAGAN MONKS.

GREAT ANTIQUITY OF MONASTICISM. As old as religion; Two sources of information, — monumental and biblical; The testimony of the former; The Sacred Books of the Ancients examined. *Chaldea.* The Nabatean Agriculture. Azada (about 4500 B.C.), the first great monk. *India.* The Vedas; The Law of Manu examined; Its monkish character; Gotama Buddha; Examination of the monkish code called the Winaya Pitaka. *Persia.* The Zend-Avesta. *China.* The Chou-King; Confucius a monk. *Greece.* The Order founded by Pythagoras; the Pagan Jesuits; Monasticism as it exists to-day in the East; Striking similarity between Hindoo monks and those of Christendom.

THE origin of monasticism will always be enveloped in mystery. "Its history is shrouded in the same obscurity as the source of the mighty streams upon the banks of which the first ascetics commenced the practice of

[1] D. Chwolson. Ueber die Ueberreste der altbabylonischen Literatur. St. Petersburg, 1859 (reviewed by Rev. O. D. Miller, in The Universalist Quarterly for July, 1869). M. le Baron de Sainte Croix. Recherches Historiques et Critiques sur les Mystères du Paganisme. Paris, 1817. R. Spence Hardy. Eastern Monachism. London, 1850.

their austerities." It has been remarked, in the previous chapter, that men had no sooner begun to come together in society, than individuals began to separate themselves from it, and sought the solitude and idleness. Some were led to take this step on account of a contemplative disposition; others because they were too proud to bend themselves to the extent which is necessitated when men dwell together, or too indolent to discharge the duties which society imposes, or too sensitive to sustain the sight of those evils which it involves. The former class was always comparatively small; for, as has been well said, "man is, naturally, more social than any bee." It should be confessed, however, that, in remote antiquity, we find sages and philosophers following this mode of life. Voltaire says, "The older a nation is, just so much older is its religion;"[1] and we may add, "The older the religion, the older its ascetic prac-

[1] No man was ever less an atheist than Voltaire. He asserts at least forty times in his voluminous works, that there

tices;" for they were among the first forms assumed by the religious impulse, and not among the later and better ones. They belong to the religion of the passions and emotion, and not to the religion of reason Monasticism, then, is as old as religion itself; for it does not gain favor with the progress of new ideas, but is gradually falling in the estimation of all.

In accordance with this view of our subject, we begin the search after the origin of asceticism by examining the most ancient records of the human race which can be found.

There are two sources from which our information may be drawn, — first, the inscrip-

has never been a race or tribe in the history of the world which did not believe in the existence of a Supreme Being. The Jesuits and the atheists were the particular objects of his irony. The former, in order to protect themselves, denounced Voltaire to the people as an atheist, and forbade them to read his works. If one questioned the doctrine of the immaculate conception, or rebuked the corrupt practices of the priesthood in times gone by, these guardians of the public morality lost no time in blackening his character, so that no one should dare to examine his writings.

tions which have been discovered in South-western Asia and Egypt; second, the sacred and historical books of ancient peoples. Until quite recently, the former, which is the older record, has remained a sealed volume to us; but, since the beginning of the last century, much has been done towards deciphering its contents. Ultimately, these remains must afford a vast fund of information concerning the manners, customs, politics, and religions of the nations to whom we are indebted for them. The inscriptions found in Assyrian and Mesopotamian ruins, alone, amount to "whole libraries of annals and works of science and literature." Sir Henry Rawlinson puts forth this statement: "On the clay tablets which we have found at Nineveh, and which now are to be counted by thousands, there are explanatory treatises on almost every subject under the sun." It is to be understood, however, that only an exceedingly small portion of these inscriptions has as yet been deciphered.

Fortunately, many of them are written in three languages, Assyrian, Persian, and Scythian: the last two very much resembling the dialects now spoken in Persia and Scythia; and to this last circumstance, we are indebted for our knowledge of Chaldean hieroglyphics.

In Egypt, a fortunate accident gave us the key to the hieroglyphics of that country. In 1799, a French artillery officer discovered, near the village of Rosetta, a stone which bore three inscriptions. The upper one was in hieroglyphics, the middle in enchorial or popular characters, and the lower in Greek. This invaluable tablet afterwards fell into the hands of Sir William R. Hamilton, by whom it was placed in the British Museum, instead of the Louvre as had been originally intended.[1]

The tablets discovered at Nineveh and in Egypt, abound in representations of priests and religious ceremonies. We know that many of the priests shaved their heads, and wore always a peculiar habit, which, in early

[1] Bunsen, Egypt's Place in Universal History.

historic times, we are told was white. They taught that the body must be kept pure by fasting and other ascetic observances. Their diet was very severe, and beans were particularly abhorred (for sanitary reasons, it is presumed). Pythagoras, who visited Egypt, borrowed this antipathy, and introduced it into the rules of his order, as will hereafter appear. Herodotus informs us, that after a battle the heads of the Egyptians were found to be almost as hard as a stone, while those of the Persians were so soft that they could be fractured with ease. From infancy, the former practised shaving the head, while the latter were accustomed to wear a kind of head-dress.

The information which we are able to glean from monumental sources is exceedingly meagre; but if the "rock-cut temples" of Arabia and India could speak to us, we might expect to hear a story of midnight vigils, macerations of the body, long-protracted silence and meditation. Nearly 600 B.C., the artificial caves of India were occupied by Buddhistical monks; and there is conclusive evidence that they had served the Brahmins for a like purpose. The manner of their construction leads to the supposition that they were originally intended for monkish abodes; and, if so, the exceeding great antiquity of monasticism can no longer be doubted. These temples and caves are the oldest monuments of the countries in which they are found.

For exact and reliable information, however, we are obliged to resort to the written books of the ancients. For many centuries it has been known that there existed a work, in Arabic translations, called "The Nabatean Agriculture," which was capable of throwing great light upon the history of ancient Babylon. Scholars have frequently alluded to it in a general way; but it remained for a celebrated German critic to give the world a tolerably comprehensive idea of its contents. Professor Chwolson published the results of his researches at St. Petersburg in 1859; and both Max Müller and Ernest Renan have also examined the work in a cursory manner. It seems to have been written at Babylon about the time of Nebuchadnezzar, or 600 B.C.; and some idea of its extensiveness may be formed from the statement of Professor Chwolson, who says that it would make more than 2,400 quarto pages.

Here we find a careful history of Chaldea, which reaches back nearly, if not quite, five thousand years before the beginning of our era. It has long been maintained, that Abraham was a Chaldean; and hence the history of the Jews down to his time, was probably borrowed from that of his native country.[1] We are not surprised, then, to find in this work a

[1] Sir Henry Rawlinson is reported to have announced, at the last meeting of the Royal Asiatic Society, that such progress has been made in the collection and arrangement of the Nineveh inscribed fragments, as to make it beyond doubt that they would be able to derive the whole of the history given in the book of Genesis, down to the time of Abraham, from these ancient documents. The Babylonian documents give a very exact geographical account of the Garden of Eden, and amply illustrate the Flood and the Tower of Babel.

circumstantial account of a great man by the name of Adami, the whole description of whose character, as well as the time in which he lived, justifies us in identifying him with the Adam of Gen. ii. 19, 20. Mr. Miller says, in his interesting article already alluded to, "But the more we examine the works before us from Professor Chwolson's pen, the stronger grow our suspicions that many of the persons alluded to by Qutami (author of The Nabatean Agriculture), are identical with the biblical patriarchs of similar name; differently dressed up, it is true, and playing a somewhat different *rôle*, from what we find in the book of Genesis."

It seems to us more probable, that the Jews borrowed their characters from the Chaldeans, and not *vice versa*. Abraham brought Adam with him from Chaldea, as the Priests and the Levites brought the devil out of the Babylonian captivity. The Jews were a nation of borrowers; borrowed from everybody with whom they came in contact, and lent to no one. The Jewish religion was a close corporation in more than one sense of the word.

Long before Adami, however, there appears to us the noble image of Azada, apostle of Saturn; and we are informed that he "founded the religion of renunciation or asceticism." "His partisans and followers were the subjects of persecution by the higher and cultivated classes; but to the mass of the people, on the contrary, they were the objects of the highest veneration." Such has always been the lot of the monks. We are forced to believe that Azada was no more the founder of Chaldean asceticism, than Buddha was of that of India, or St. Benedict of that of Christendom; but he is the first great monk of whom we have any account, since planet-worship is the oldest form of religion that is known.

This work carries us still farther back into antiquity; never once abandoning, however, the path of strictly historical times, and, at the highest point, shows us a people who were civilized and employed the arts.

Dhagrit, who lived about 2000 B.C., was undoubtedly an advocate of ascetic life. He inveighs against the godlessness of those who believed it possible to preserve the human body from decay after death by the employment of certain natural agents. "Not by natural means," warmly replies Dhagrit, "can man preserve his body from corruption and dissolution after death: but only through good deeds, *religious exercises*, and offering of sacrifices, by invoking the gods by their great and beautiful names; *by prayers during the night, and fasts during the day.*" Thus Dhagrit goes on, in his pious zeal, to give the names of various saints of Babylonian antiquity, whose bodies had long been preserved after death from corruption and change, and says, "These men had distinguished themselves by piety, by abstemiousness, and by their manner of life, which resembled that of angels; and the gods, therefore, by their grace, had preserved the bodies of these men from corruption; whereby those of later times, in view of the same, were encouraged in piety, and in the imitation of those holy modes of life."[1] All of this reminds one very much of St. Francis Xavier, the Jesuit missionary, whose body was wonderfully preserved a long time after his death.

Thus far, the sources from which we have drawn our information are but little known, and their complete reliability may possibly be called in question. From this point, however, we shall make use of none but the most reliable authority, and our conclusions will rest upon historical records of unquestionable character.

The oldest books in existence, not including the Hebrew Scriptures, are the Veda[2] and the Law of Manu[3] (sacred books of the Brahmins), the Zend-Avesta (sacred book of the

[1] We employ Mr. Miller's translation, since the original text is not now at hand.

[2] Rig Veda, translated by H. H. Wilson, London, 1850.

[3] Les Livres Sacrés de l'Orient, G. Pauthier, Paris, 1840.

Persians or Zoroastrians),[1] and the Chou-King[2] (sacred book of China).

In addition to these, we have the Tripitaka, three baskets (sacred book of the Buddhists), which is little more than a manual of monkish usages, committed to writing about 100 B.C. There is some doubt as to which is the older, — the Hebrew Scriptures or some portions of the Rig-Veda.

With these new sources of information, let us continue, then, our examination. With regard to the early Brahminical writings, we find that to be true which we should have naturally expected. The Rig-Veda, portions of which may be assigned to a period not later than 2400 B.C., consists mainly of hymns and prayers: it is a liturgy. This must have always been the first form of sacred literature. Notwithstanding this fact, many parts of the work bear the stamp of asceticism ; and moreover, as has been observed by Mr. Hardy,

1 Zend-Avesta von Spiegel, Leipzig.

2 Les Livres Sacrés de l'Orient, G. Pauthier, Paris, 1840.

"The practice of asceticism is so interwoven with Brahminism, under all the phases it has assumed, that we cannot realize its existence apart from the principles of the ascetic."[1] At an early period of the present era of manifestation, Dhruva, the son of Uttanapada, the son of Manu Swayambhuva, who was "born of and one with Brahma," began to perform penance, *as enjoined by the sages*, on the banks of the Yamuna. While his mind was wholly absorbed in meditation, the mighty Hari, identical with all natures, took possession of his heart. Vishnu being thus present in his mind, the earth, the supporter of elemental life, could not sustain the weight of the ascetic.

"The celestials called Yamas, being excessively alarmed, then took counsel with Indra how they should interrupt the devout exercises of Dhruva; and the divine beings termed Kushmandas, in company with their king,

[1] It should be remembered, too, that Brahminism is probably much older than its written records.

commenced anxious efforts to distract his meditations. One, assuming the semblance of his mother, Suniti, stood weeping before him, and calling in tender accents, 'My son, my son, desist from destroying thy strength by this fearful penance? What hast thou, a child but five years old, to do with rigorous penance? Desist from such fearful practices, that yield no beneficial fruit. First comes the season of youthful pastime; and when that is over, it is the time for study: then succeeds the period of worldly enjoyments; and lastly, that of austere devotion. This is thy season of pastime, my child. Hast thou engaged in these practices to put an end to existence? Thy chief duty is love for me: duties are according to time of life. Lose not thyself in bewildering error: desist from such unrighteous actions. If not, if thou wilt not desist from these austerities, I will terminate my life before thee.'

"But Dhruva, being wholly intent on seeing Vishnu, beheld not his mother weeping in his presence, and calling upon him; and the illusion crying out, 'Fly, fly, my child: the hideous spirits of ill are crowding into this terrible forest with uplifted weapons,' quickly disappeared. Then advanced frightful rakshasas, wielding terrible arms, and with countenances emitting fiery flame; and nocturnal fiends thronged around the prince, uttering fearful noises, and whirling and tossing their threatening weapons. Hundreds of jackals from whose mouths gushed flame, as they devoured their prey, were howling around, to appall the boy, wholly engrossed by meditation. The goblins called out, 'Kill him, kill him; cut him to pieces; eat him, eat him;' and monsters, with the faces of camels and crocodiles and lions, roared and yelled, with horrible cries, to terrify the prince. But all these uncouth speeches, appalling cries, and threatening weapons, made no impression upon his senses, whose mind was completely intent on Govinda. The son of the monarch of the earth, engrossed by one idea, beheld uninterruptedly Vishnu seated in his soul, and saw no other object."

This description would apply admirably to the Christian monks who inhabited the Thebaid. The desert has always been the abode of asceticism, whose devotees, in their struggle against the flesh, peopled its sands with horrible monsters of every kind, — with devils, hobgoblins, and giants, — who (in the minds of the people) have held possession ever since.

The Vedas commanded that the tonsure should be performed; but, so far as known, it prescribes no rules with regard to the monastic life. It should be kept in mind, however, that only a small portion of the work has yet been translated. The four Vedas, when collected, form eleven huge quarto volumes; while the Rig-Veda — which has been translated in part, by Wilson — is contained in a single duodecimo of about five hundred pages.

It is not until we reach the "Law of Manu," that our feet touch firm ground. Now we know where we are. The exact time when this work was committed to writing cannot be determined. Sir Wm. Jones says 800 B.C.; and Max Müller remarks that it is the only work in Sanscrit the early date of which, assigned to it by Sir William Jones, from the first, has not been assailed. It is, without doubt, much older than this. The absence of any mention of the doctrine of the Trinity would assign it to a date at least 1000 B.C.; and the rules which it contains for the conduct of monastic life must have been in use many ages before they were committed to writing. A large portion of this work is taken up by regulations to be observed by those who wish to attain to the ultimate good by the practice of monastic observances. The rule of St. Benedict itself does not afford a more decided proof of the existence of the ascetic life. It is divided into twelve books. The Sixth Book is entitled "Duties of the Anchorite and of the Ascetic Devotee." The subject of the Eleventh Book is "Penitences and

Expiations." The Dwidjas, for whom these rules are principally laid down, are described as a sort of monk who wore tonsure, girdle, carried staff, asked alms, fasted, lacerated the body, and dwelt, for the most part, in the deserts and forests. We have space but for a few illustrations, which will suffice, however, to show the character of this work. As Sir William Jones's translation is not at hand, we render a few passages from that of M. Deslongchamps, a French scholar of considerable note. From the Sixth Book, "Duties of the Anchorite and of the Ascetic Devotee," we quote as follows: —

¶ 24. The Dwidja, who dwells alone, should deliver himself to austerities, increasing constantly in their severity, that he may wither up his mortal substance.

¶ 27. Let him receive from the Brahminical anchorites, who live in houses, such alms as may be necessary to support his existence.[1]

[1] The case was similar in early Christian times. Simon the Stylite, and a host of others, were thus provided for.

¶ 49. Meditating with delight on the supreme soul, seated, wanting nothing, inaccessible to all sensual desire, without other society than his own soul, let him live here below in the constant expectancy of the eternal beatitude.

¶ 75. In subduing his organs, in accomplishing the pious duties prescribed by the Vedas, and in submitting one's self to the most austere practices, one is able to attain, here below, to the supreme end; which is to become identified with Brahma.[1]

¶ 87. The novice, the married man, the anchorite, and the ascetic devotee, form four distinct orders, which derive their origin from the superior of the house.

¶ 91. The Dwidjas who belong to these four orders ought always to practise with the greatest care, the ten virtues which compose their duty.

¶ 92. Resignation, the act of rendering good for evil, temperance, probity, purity, the subjugation of the senses, the knowledge of the Sastras, that of the

[1] Their whole doctrine of spirit, of the Supreme Being, and the relation of man to God, must have made the Brahmins ascetics from the very first. So that, when the origin of this religion can be ascertained, we may say, without further examination, Monasticism was there, and gave birth to it.

supreme soul, veracity, and abstinence from choler; such are the ten virtues in which their duty consists.

From the Eleventh Book, "Penitences and Expiations," we make the following extracts: —

¶ 211. The Dwidja who undergoes the *ordinary* penitence, called Pradjapatya, ought to eat, during three days, only in the morning; during the next three days only at night; during the following three days, he should partake only of such food as persons may give him voluntarily, without his begging for it; and, finally, let him fast three days entirely.

¶ 214. A Brahmin, accomplishing the *severe* penitence (Taptakritchhra), ought to swallow nothing but warm water, warm milk, cold clarified butter, and warm vapor, employing each of them three days in succession.

¶ 215. He who, master of his senses and perfectly attentive, supports a fast of twelve days, makes the penitence called Paroka, which expiates all of his faults.

¶ 216. Let the penitent who desires to make the Tchandrayana, having eaten fifteen mouthfuls on the day of the full moon, diminish his nourishment by one mouthful each day during the fifteen days of obscuration which follow, in such a manner, that, on the fourteenth day, he shall eat but one mouthful; and then let him fast on the fifteenth, which is the day of the new moon; let him augment, on the contrary, his nourishment by one mouthful each day, during the next fifteen days, commencing the first day with one mouthful.

¶ 239. Great criminals, and all other men guilty of diverse faults, are released from the consequences of their sins by austerities practised with exactitude.

¶ 251. By reciting the Hovichyantiya or the Natamanha sixteen times a day for a month, or by repeating, inaudibly, the hymn Poroucha, he who has defiled the bed of his spiritual master is absolved from all fault.

The Vanaprastha were Brahminical anchorites who inhabited the deserts, lived on vegetables, devoted themselves to contemplation, macerated the body, fought with devils and giants (as a natural consequence), and were insensible to heat and cold. As the procreation of at least one child is strictly enjoined by Brahminism, some took their wives along, but never had intercourse with them except at such times as they were most likely to conceive. They consumed disgusting things, and left the deserts only to beg. They were called later by the Greeks Gymnosophists; and, notwithstanding they went perfectly naked, no throb or involuntary movement was ever seen in any part of their bodies.[1] Women who were barren oftentimes came and touched their shrivelled member, hoping thereby to become fruitful. Not the slightest emotion was noticed at such times. These old ascetics would have regarded with contempt the practices of Christian monks, who were, indeed, children when compared with their Eastern ancestors.

What St. Benedict became to the monks of Christendom, Gotama Buddha was to those

[1] Description of the Character, Manners, and Customs of the People of India, by the Abbé J. A. Dubois, Phil., 1818.

of India. Eleven hundred and fifty-three years before the former enunciated his law from the top of Mont Cassim, — that Sinai of western monasticism, — Buddha, the Moses of eastern monachism, was born at Kapilawastu. Up to this time the Brahminical ascetics had been without a settled rule or organization. The Law of Manu specified the manner of conducting many austere observances; but each monastery was accustomed to arrange its own inner life and stood quite independent of any other.

The growth of monasticism was something after this manner. First came austere practices without separation from society: then the devotee sought the solitude; this form was that of the anchorite (*αναχώρειν*, to retire.) Some one who was particularly celebrated for the holiness of his life, or more inventive than others in methods of bodily torment, soon began to gather admirers and imitators about him. They came and dug their caves or built their huts in the neighborhood of his;

and gave to him, in early Christian times, the name of abbas, or father. Thus arose the second form of life, and those who followed it were called cenobites (*κοίνος*, common; *βίος*, life.)

Sometimes the community was assembled under one roof; at other times, as in the Thebiad, they dwelt apart. As yet, however, their mode of life was by no means settled or uniform. Now was the time for a law-giver; and the people of India found theirs in the person of Buddha (the Enlightened), who was born 624 B.C.

He manifested early a love for contemplation, and was determined to the ascetic mode of life by seeing a monk who carried an alms-bowl, and whose external appearance spoke of inward peace and composure. His father was king of Kapilawastu, who, having detected the dreamer in his son, married him, while yet quite young, to a princess who gave birth to a child before Buddha divorced himself from her. The circumstances which led him to take this step are thus narrated by J. Barthélemy Saint Hilaire.[1]

"One day when the prince, with a large retinue, was driving through the eastern gate of the city, on the way to one of his parks, he met on the road an old man, broken and decrepit. One could see the veins and muscles over the whole of his body; his teeth chattered; he was covered with wrinkles, bald, and hardly able to utter hollow and unmelodious sounds. He was bent on his stick; and all his limbs and joints trembled. 'Who is that man?' said the prince to his coachman. 'He is small and weak; his flesh and his blood are dried up; his muscles stick to his skin; his head is white; his teeth chatter; his body is wasted away; leaning on his stick he is hardly able to walk, stumbling at every step. Is there something peculiar in his family, or is this the common lot of all created beings?'

"'Sir,' replied the coachman, 'that man is sinking under old age; his senses have become obtuse, suffering has destroyed his strength, and he is despised by his relations. He is without support and useless;

[1] Le Buddha et sa Religion.

and people have abandoned him, like a dead tree in a forest. But this is not peculiar to his family. In every creature, youth is defeated by old age. Your father, your mother, all your relations, all your friends, will come to the same state: this is the appointed end of all creatures.'

"'Alas!' replied the prince, 'are creatures so ignorant, so weak, and so foolish, as to be proud of the youth by which they are intoxicated, not seeing the old age which awaits them? As for me, I go away. Coachman, turn my chariot quickly. What have I, — the future prey of old age, — what have I to do with pleasure?' And the young prince returned to the city without going to his park.

"Another time the prince was driving through the southern gate to his pleasure-garden, when he perceived on the road a man suffering from illness, parched with fever, his body wasted, covered with mud, without a friend, without a home, hardly able to breathe, and frightened at the sight of himself and the approach of death. Having questioned his coachman, and received from him the answer which he expected, the young prince said, 'Alas! health is but the sport of a dream, and the fear of suffering must take this frightful form. Where is the wise man who, after having seen what he is, could any longer think of joy and pleasure?' The prince turned his chariot and returned to the city.

"A third time he was driving to his pleasure-garden through the western gate, when he saw a dead body on the road, lying on a bier, and covered with a cloth. The friends stood about, crying, sobbing, tearing their hair, covering their heads with dust, striking their breasts, and uttering wild cries. The prince, again calling his coachman to witness this painful scene, exclaimed, 'Oh, woe to the youth, which must be destroyed by old age! Woe to health, which must be destroyed by so many diseases! Woe to this life, where a man remains so short a time! If there were no old age, no disease, no death; if these could be made captive for ever!' Then, betraying for the first time his intentions, the young prince said, 'Let us turn back: I must think how to accomplish deliverance.'

"A last meeting put an end to his hesitation. He was driving through the northern gate on the way to his pleasure-gardens, when he saw a mendicant who appeared outwardly calm, subdued, looking downwards, wearing with an air of dignity his religious vestment, and carrying an alms-bowl. 'Who is this man?' asked the prince. 'Sir,' replied the coachman, 'this man is one of those who are called *bhikshus*, or mendicants. He has renounced all pleasures, all desires, and leads a life of austerity. He tries to conquer himself. He has become a devotee: without passion, without envy, he walks about asking for alms?'

"'This is good and well said,' replied the prince. 'The life of a devotee has always been praised by the wise. It will be my refuge, and the refuge of other creatures: it will lead us to a real life, to happiness and immortality.'

"With these words, the young prince turned his chariot, and returned to the city."[1]

Buddha then declared to his father and wife his determination to become a recluse, and soon after escaped from his palace in the night while the guards had fallen asleep.

The religion which he established, after a lapse of two thousand years, is now professed

[1] Translated in Müller's Essays on the Science of Religion.

by one-third of the inhabitants of the entire globe. One king is said to have founded eighty-four thousand monasteries for his order, that being the number of discourses which Buddha pronounced during his lifetime. The "Law" which he gave his order is contained in the first of the three Pitakas, and was orally handed down until about 100 B.C., when it was committed to writing in the island of Ceylon. It is called the Winaya Pitaka, and contains rules for every conceivable monastic observance. It is composed of forty-two thousand two hundred and fifty stanzas. To alms-giving Buddha attached an extraordinary importance. He declares that "there is no reward either in this world or in the next that may not be received through alms-giving." Ten centuries later, Chrysostom wrote, "Hast thou a penny? purchase heaven. Heaven is on sale, and in the market, and yet ye mind it not! Give a crust, and take back paradise; give the least, and receive the greatest; give the perishable, and receive the imperishable; give the corruptible, and receive the incorruptible. Alms are the redemption of the soul. . . . Alms-giving which is able to break the chain of thy sins. . . . Alms-giving, the queen of virtues, and the readiest of all ways of getting into heaven, and the best advocated there."[1] According to the Winaya Pitaka, "The wise priest never asks for any thing; he disdains to beg: it is a proper object for which he carries the alms-bowl; and this is the only mode of solicitation." Celibacy, poverty, the tonsure, a particular garb, confession of sins, &c., are made compulsory. The vows, however, are not taken for life; and a monk may retire from the order if he finds it impossible to remain continent. A novitiate is provided for; and there are "Nuns" or "Sisters" who live in houses by themselves.

The novice usually begins her connection with the order in the school, where she is sent while yet quite young. Foundlings

[1] Taylor's Ancient Christianity.

were often given to the early Christian monasteries, by whom they were reared for the ascetic life. No Buddhist can attain to Nirwana, unless he has served a time as an ascetic.

There are five modes of meditation specified by the Pitaka,—1. Maitri; 2. Mudita; 3. Karuna; 4. Upeksha; 5. Asubha. We read of a monk who was so profoundly sunk in contemplation, that he did not wash his feet for thirty years; so that at last the divine beings, called *dervas*, could smell him a thousand miles off.

The monk refrains from severely injuring his body; so that he may practise, as long as possible, his ascetic rites. Their mode of reasoning on this subject is illustrated by the following quotation from the Milinda-prasna, a work in Pali and Singhalese:—

Milinda. "Do the priests respect the body?"—*Nagasena.* "No."—*Milinda.* "Then why do they take so much pains to preserve it? Do they not by this means say, 'This is me, or mine'?" — *Nagasena.* "Were you ever wounded by an arrow in battle?" — *Milinda.* "Yes." — *Nagasena.* "Was not the wound anointed? Was it not rubbed with oil? And was it not covered with a soft bandage?" — *Milinda.* "Yes." — *Nagasena.* "Was this done because you respected the wound, or took delight in it?" — *Milinda.* "No; but that it might be healed." — *Nagasena.* "In like manner, the priests do not preserve the body because they respect it, but that they may have the power required for the keeping of the precepts."

The Zend-Avesta, written about 500 B.C., contains, so far as we have been able to discover from a hurried examination, no allusion to ascetic rites; but this fact would go no farther to disprove the existence of monastic life among the Persians, than the absence of such allusion from the New Testament would disprove the existence of Jewish monks. This work is not of an historical character; and what was said about the Vedas is particularly true of it, — prayers and hymns make up almost its entire contents. The followers of Zoroaster originally dwelt with the Brahminical or Sanscrit branch of the Aryan family; and we know that monasticism was rife among them before the separation took place. It is not likely that they ever shook off this institution, which is as universal as religion or drunkenness. We are told that there was a class of "solitaries" among them.

"According to the Desatir, the Dobistan, and the old Iranian histories, there was a great king of that branch of the Aryan people known as Kai-Khuero, who was a prophet and an ascetic. He had no children; and, after a 'glorious reign of sixty years,' he abdicated in favor of a subordinate prince, also an ascetic, who, after a long reign, resigned his throne to his son Gushtasp. It was during the reign of Gushtasp that Zoroaster appeared. Gushtasp was succeeded by Bohman, his grandson." These were not kings of Persia, but they reigned at Balkh, and lived many centuries before Persia became an independent kingdom. This would place the origin of asceticism anterior to Zoroaster, who lived, the Greeks said, five thousand years before the Trojan war, or six thousand before Plato,— an antiquity greater than that assigned to it by the "Nabatean Agriculture."

An examination of the Chou-King, the sacred book *par excellence* of China, is without fruit for our purpose. It is a significant fact, however, that the word "priest" is written in Chinese "Cha-men," or "Sang-men," which mean, respectively, one who exerts himself,[1] or one who restrains himself. The Chou-King was transcribed by Confucius[2] about 480 B.C., and to him we owe its preservation. It is only one out of a large number of books, upon religious topics, which must have existed in his time. Lao-Kiün, who lived several generations before Confu-

[1] Remarkable similarity between the derivation of this word and that of ascetic (from *ασκεῖν*, to exercise, or practise gymnastics).

[2] Life and Teachings of Confucius, by James Legge, D.D. Phila., 1867.

cius, was a great ascetic, advocated perfect freedom from passions, and passed much of his time in the mountains. It is known that Confucius taught no new doctrines, but insisted upon a more faithful observation of the ancient law.[1] He was born 550 B.C., and died 478 B.C. At nineteen years of age he divorced himself from his wife, after she had given birth to a son, to devote himself to study and meditation; and his last days were passed in a quiet valley, where he retired with a few of his followers. He fasted quite frequently, and advocated many other monkish observances; such as retirement, contemplation, and agricultural employment. (Schott, Werke des chinesischen Weisen Kong-Fu Dsü. Halle, 1826. Compare also Meng Tseu ed. Stanislaus Julien l. 1, c. 5, par. 29; c. 6, p. 29.)

Mencius, an apostle of Confucius, born 400 B.C., says, "Though a man may be wicked,

[1] It is a fact worthy of notice that the man who, perhaps, resembled Jesus Christ the most of any one in history, should have laid no claims whatever to originality.

yet if he adjust his thoughts, fast, and bathe, he may sacrifice to God."

Of Grecian monasticism, until the time of Pythagoras, we can now ascertain but very little. It was borrowed, without doubt, from the Egyptians. The mysteries of Bacchus and Ceres were copied after those of Osiris and Isis. These latter, in some respects, resembled Freemasonry more than they did monastic orders. They forbade, however, all sensuous enjoyment, enjoined contemplation, long-protracted silence, &c. Moreover, it is probable that Pythagoras found here many of those ascetic observances which he afterwards introduced into his own order. Bunsen says that the rules for the conduct of Egyptian priests, as described by Chæremon and preserved by Porphyry, remind one of the Law of Manu and the Vedas.

More than two thousand years before Ignatius Loyola assembled the nucleus of his great "Society" in a subterranean chapel in the city of Paris, there was founded at Crotona in

Greece an order of monks whose principles, constitution, aims, methods, and final end entitle them to be called, I think, the "Pagan Jesuits." This institution owed its origin to Pythagoras, who was born at Samos about 600 B.C.[1] Until fifty years of age, his time was employed in travelling in foreign countries and preparing to found his order, during which time he visited almost every part of the known world. Having returned to the island of Samos, he began at first to lead the life of an anchorite, passing much of his time in a solitary cave. Among the masses, he was held in the greatest reverence. One day he bought a net full of fish from a fisherman, and then threw them all back into the sea again, saying that it was wrong to kill fish. To this the people added, that he gave the exact number of the fish while the net was yet under water. He was reported, at other

1 Pythagoras und die Pythagorasage, Eduard Zeller in his Vorträge und Abhandlung. Leipzig, 1865. For a more full account of Pythagoras and his doctrine, see the works of Barthélemy, Meiner, Hissmann, Tiedmann, Tenneman, and Buhle.

times, to have healed the sick, raised the dead, stilled the waves of the sea with a word, and it was said that he gave himself out for Apollo, who had assumed the human form.

Pythagoras employed still several years in preparing to found his order, which was called the Pythagorean Union or Fraternity. The cloister at Crotona may be regarded as the first monastery or as the Abbey of this order, from whence all the other branches derived their authority. There were three hundred members in this house alone; while others were rapidly established all over Greece, as well as in Carthage, Cyrene, Sicily, and Africa. The three vows of poverty, chastity, and obedience, were imposed. A novitiate, which lasted three years, was provided. The wearing of a certain garb was compulsory; and the institution possessed altogether a monkish character. On being admitted into the house, the novice gave up all the money or other valuables which he possessed; he was treated with the greatest indifference; he was not favored with a single look, and was left entirely to himself.[1]

The severest punishment ever inflicted was expulsion from the order, when the money paid on entering was returned to the expelled, and a gravestone was erected for him, to show that he was dead to the order.

Since physical action is necessary to the preservation of the health, gymnastic exercises were introduced; and hence, probably, the name which was afterwards applied to them (ἀσκηταί, athletes). That there was no considerable difference between their mode of life, and that of early Christian monks,[2] is shown

[1] How much this resembles the treatment of early Christian novices. "Isidore, an Egyptian monk, when asking to be admitted into the house, said to the abbot, 'I am in your hands, as iron in the hands of the smith.' The abbot ordered him to remain without the gate, and to prostrate himself at the feet of every one who passed by, begging prayers for his soul, as for a leper. This command he obeyed, and remained in this humiliating position for the space of seven years. The first year he had a violent conflict; the second, tranquillity; and the third, pleasure." — (Hardy.)

[2] Each monastery prided itself on keeping several athletes, who often disguised themselves and went to places

by the fact that the name *ascetic* was inherited by the latter, and remains in use even to this day.

Among the followers of Pythagoras, there was an order of females, called "Sisters;" whose care was entrusted to his daughter.

Some of the observances prescribed by him were quite peculiar. From time to time, a delicious banquet was prepared. All the monks seated themselves at the table, and enjoyed for a while the sight and odor of the viands; then every one arose, without having touched the dishes, sent the food to the slaves, and fasted the whole day.

For beans they had an unutterable horror. They preferred to suffer death rather than even touch them. Long after the death of Pythagoras, Dionysius, tyrant of Syracuse, desired to see some Pythagoreans and converse with them, perhaps for the purpose of

where games were being celebrated, and, having surpassed all competitors, threw aside their mask, thus exposing their monkish garb to view. They returned to the monastery, and related the incident with great relish.

discovering the members of that order in his own kingdom. With this object in view, he sent a body of troops into Greece, who fell upon twelve persons in the vicinity of Metapont, the character of whom was betrayed by their garb. The soldiers immediately gave chase to the strangers, who promptly took to flight, and would undoubtedly have made their escape, had not the way been obstructed by a large field of beans. Brought to bay, they stubbornly resisted until all but two of their number (an old man, and a woman great with child) were cut down. These latter were carried to Syracuse; but since no information could be gained from them concerning the order to which they belonged, Dionysius caused them to be put to the rack. Upon this the woman bit off her tongue for fear that she might be weak enough to divulge that which she ought not, and the man remained silent until the last. It is possible that their abstinence from beans, without any alleged reason, was merely to illustrate thereby more clearly their implicit obedience to their rule.

That which constituted their particular resemblance to the "Society of Jesus," was the great emphasis which they placed upon the duty of obedience to superiors, their opposition to democratic institutions, their political intrigue, and their fate. They had, likewise, "Lay Brethren," who mingled in active life.

Pythagoras was the General of the Order, towards whom all of the members manifested the most blind and implicit obedience. The words "He said it" were regarded in the same light as one of their mathematical demonstrations; and they swore by no higher name than that of their "Master" (*jurare in verba magistri*). The order, like that of the Jesuits, was founded on monarchial principles; and the wave of democracy swept it away. All of the most ancient writers agree that the Pythagoreans made themselves obnoxious by their attempts to alter the constitutions, in the countries where they were established, against the will of the people and to the detriment of their rights.

A similar policy afterwards pursued by the Jesuits, caused them to be driven out of Catholic Bavaria and Switzerland;[1] while but recently in Spain, casting their lot, as usual, with the cause of absolute monarchy, they have shared its fate. Their political intrigues have resulted in their expulsion from every European country.

In Crotona itself, the storm against the Pythagoreans first broke out. As the order was assembled to confer concerning the conduct of a war, the monastery was surrounded by the populace and set on fire. Pythagoras escaped; but the greater number of his followers perished in the flames. He wandered over many countries, "warned off" wherever he went, and finished his life, at a very advanced age, in a temple at Metapont, where he fled

[1] An article inserted in the Constitution of Switzerland, with the consent and by the desire of the Catholic Cantons, forbids the Jesuits establishing themselves in the country.

for protection, — some say murdered, others say starved.

It is probable that the Pythagoreans owed their untimely end, not alone to their monarchial principles, but to their evident intention of placing themselves in possession of the reins of government, as did the Jesuits in Paraguay. The resemblance goes still farther. After the destruction of the order, and the death of its founder, many attempts were made to re-establish it, in spite of the hatred of the people and the mistrust of rulers. The ex-Pythagoreans conducted themselves with the utmost discretion, and cultivated the strictest morality. The most learned among them continued their researches, and left many valuable writings to posterity. Their philosophical mantle, however, fell upon a new school, among whom Epaminondas and Plato are usually reckoned.

Having now completed the general survey of ancient asceticism, let us glance for a moment at this phase of life as it has existed among the inhabitants of India in recent times.

The "Law of Manu," as has already been shown, contains rules for nearly all the monkish observances; such as the tonsure, fasting, celibacy, mendicancy, novitiate, &c. We are told that Hindoo devotees "swing on hooks in honor of Siva; hang themselves by the feet, head-downwards, over a fire; roll on a bed of prickly thorns; jump on a couch filled with sharp knives; bore holes in their tongues, and stick their bodies full of pins and needles."[1] Some of the "Fakirs" (Arabic, *fakhar*, poor) hold their arms so long in one position that they become permanently stiffened; and those who stretch their hands up over their heads lose the power to lower them. Others bend their bodies until they crook at a right angle; and there are those who keep the hand clasped together so long that the nails grow into the flesh and come out on the other side. Some

[1] Article on Brahminism, by Dr. J. F. Clarke, in Atlantic Monthly, May, 1869.

of them never sit or lie down, but are supported by a rope placed for that purpose; others lay fire upon their head, and thus burn the scalp to the bone. Hassan al Bassri says, a fakir resembles a dog in nine things, —

1st, He is always hungry.

2d, He has no sure abiding place.

3d, He watches by night.

4th, He never abandons his master even when maltreated.

5th, He is satisfied with the lowest place.

6th, He yields his place to whoever wishes it.

7th, He loves whoever beats him.

8th, He keeps quiet while others eat.

9th, He accompanies his master without ever thinking of returning to the place which he has left.

There are, at least, 1,000,000 Mohammedan and Hindoo fakirs in India alone, besides many other religious ascetics. Some of them live isolated, sleep on the ground and go naked. Instead of wood they use dry cow-dung for making a fire: since the cow is a sacred animal among them this is regarded as a particularly meritorious practice. Another class rove about in companies. They choose a chief, — who wears a chain attached to one of his legs, — and practise the most rigid mortifications. In their weekly meetings, some of their number are always selected to hold a red-hot piece of iron between their teeth until it becomes cold; while others make deep incisions in their bodies with sharp-edged instruments.

"A fakir will sometimes take it into his head to trundle himself along like a cart-wheel for a couple of hundred miles or so. He ties his wrists to his ankles; gets a *tire*, composed of chopped straw, mud, and cow-dung, laid along the ridge of his backbone; a bamboo staff passed through the angle formed by his knees and elbows by way of an axle, — and off he goes; a brazen cup, with a bag and a *hubble-bubble*, hang like tassels at the two extremities of the axle. Thus accoutred, he often starts on a journey which will occupy him for several years. On arriving in the vicinity of a village, the whole population turn out to meet and escort him with due honors to the public well or tank, where he unbends and washes off the dust and dirt acquired by perambulating several miles of dusty road. After ascertaining, by minute inquiries, the state of the larders of the assembled villagers, he takes up his quarters with the man who is best able to entertain him. When the supplies begin to fail, he ties his hands to his heels again, gets a fresh tire put on, and is escorted out of the village with the same formalities as accompanied his entrance."[1]

D'Herbelot estimates that there were 800,000 Mohammedan[2] and 1,200,000 Hindoo fakirs in India.

"To abstract one's self from matter, to renounce the gratification of the senses, to macerate the body, is thought the true road to felicity. They torture themselves with self-inflicted torments; for the body is the great enemy of the soul's salvation, and they must beat it down by ascetic mortifications."

The world is all delusion. The Vedanta declares, —

1 Encyclopædia Britannica; Art. Fakirs.

2 The original principles of Mohammedanism were unfavorable to monastic life; and religious mendicants did not appear among them until six hundred years after Mohammed, or about the thirteenth century of our era.

"From the highest state of Brahma to the lowest condition of straw, all things are delusion."

To illustrate how far this mysticism goes among the Brahmins, we quote the following from Alger's "Oriental Poetry": —

"Ribhu and Nidagha are conversing, when the king rides by. The following dramatic dialogue ensues: 'Inform me, Nidagha, which of these is the elephant and which the king.' 'Why, Ribhu, you will observe that the elephant is underneath; the king is above him.' 'Yes; but what is meant, Nidagha, by underneath, and by above?' Nidagha knocks Ribhu down, jumps upon him, and says, 'I am above, and you are underneath.' 'Very well,' cries Ribhu, 'now tell me which is you, and which is I.'"

The "Bonzes" (from the Japanese, *busso*, which means *pious*), who live in China, Burmah, Japan, &c., are priests of Buddha. They practise celibacy, live in monasteries, shave the head, never speak in public, lead a life of contemplation, and sell "relics." There are "Bonzies" (females), who have a superior of their own sex, and profess the same virtues and way of life as the men. The education of young girls is often intrusted to them.

The first Roman-Catholic missionaries who forced their way to the East were exceedingly surprised to find such a striking resemblance between the monastic customs of Buddhism and their own church. The adoption of pageantry in public worship led to their further consternation. This perfect coincidence they never fail to attribute to the machinations of the devil. Let us translate a few paragraphs from a work published at Paris, so long ago as 1724, by "le Sieur Jovet, Chanoine de Laon,"[1] which distances Father Huc by more than a century. In speaking of the island of Ceylon, he writes, —

"There are cloisters full of monks who pray continually, and who form processions dancing and singing. They are shaved like our monks, carrying a sort of chaplet, and murmuring always some prayer.

[1] L'Histoire des Religions de Tous les Royaumes du Monde. This work may be seen in the Municipal Library of the city of Nice, France.

I have seen, in these monasteries, gilded chapels with the statues of men and women who had lived more virtuously than others. These statues are covered with cloth of gold and silver: some of them bear infants in their arms, who carry large candles, which burn night and day. The monks sometimes form a procession, going two and two. Their superior is clothed in cloth of gold, and carries a golden sceptre. They are preceded by persons bearing wax candles and lighted torches; and, before saying their prayers, they prostrate themselves upon the earth."

Again: "On *fête* days the people enter the churches; and, having lighted a small piece of wood, they place it before the image upon the altar, and then, making a low obeisance, they retire. Their monks burn incense, twice a day, before an image. The monasteries, which are always crowded, are, for the most part, situated upon mountains. Some of them contain five or six hundred monks; and, in some of the cities, there are more than five thousand. They are divided into bands of ten and twenty. The oldest commands, and inflicts punishment with blows, not to exceed twenty or thirty. These monks eat no meat or flesh, shave the face and head, and are forbidden to hold any conversation with women. After their first tonsure, a mark is made upon the arm which can never be effaced. Some of them work, and some beg; while a number receive small pensions from the government. They have always children in the monastery, who come to be taught to read and write; and, when they have attained to the age of discretion, if they wish to be shaved they can remain in the house."

Thus far the reader may imagine that a Roman-Catholic monastery is being described; but his error will immediately appear from the following sentences, which contain the principal, if not the only, difference between the two institutions:—

"As to the belief of these people, they are persuaded that he who does right will be recompensed, and that he who does wrong will be punished. Further than this, they know nothing of preaching or mysteries. They never dispute about religion: all believe the same thing; and the same practices prevail everywhere in the kingdom. Many Mohammedans live among them who enjoy entire liberty in the exercise of their religion."

The people described above belong to a heathen tribe which inhabits Oriental China, the kingdom of Coray or Corree. The same writer speaks thus of Japan:—

"The Bonzes confess their sins; and the priests occupy themselves in chanting liturgies and repeating prayers. They make a procession around a lighted chapel almost in the same manner that we do in our churches. The masses believe that the priests are charged with satisfying God for the sins of the people; and the rich give them revenues. They believe that, by the prayers of the priests, they can be saved from the torments of hell. There is a certain season when they fast: it is called 'Fingan,' and is just like 'Lent' among Christians. Their priests are 'Bonzes,' who take the vow of chastity: they eat only once a day, and then only vegetables or rice. There are many different 'sects' among them, some of which live in monasteries. Many of them beg; and people employ them to say prayers for their departed friends."

With regard to China, we are informed, that "the priests fast and do not marry.

There are four orders among them, each wearing a differently colored dress. These monks shave their heads and say 'Matins,' and perform the 'offices,' just like our monks in Europe; and in their services they make use of ornaments similar to those of our priests."

Let us hear no more of Father Huc after this. His book was so fortunate as to attract the attention of his holiness the Pope, who placed it on the *Index*, to which circumstance may be attributed much of its notoriety even among Catholics themselves. [1]

The Buddhistical monks also recite por-

[1] Father Huc's Travels in Tartary, &c. "One cannot help being struck," he says, "by the similarities between the Buddhist and Roman-Catholic ceremonials. The cross, the mitre, the *dalmatique*, the *chape* or *pluvial*, that the grand Lamas wear when travelling or performing some ceremony outside of the temple; the 'office' with two choruses, psalmody, exorcism, the censer suspended with five chains, and so constructed that it may be opened and closed at will, the benediction given by the Lamas in extending the right hand over the head of the faithful, the chaplet, ecclesiastic celibacy, spiritual retreats, the *culte*, of the saints, fasts, processions, litanies, holy water, — such are the points in which the Buddhists resemble us."

tions of their sacred writings in the Pali language, which is entirely unknown to the most of them. This ceremony is called, "saying *bana*," and resembles almost exactly a Catholic Mass. Laymen attend, who go away with the consciousness of having acquired merit by listening to it. "One by one each day, in regular order, the *samanera* novices shall kindle a fire, light a lamp, make all ready for the reading of the *bana*, call the priest who is appointed to recite it, wash his feet, sit down in an orderly manner and listen to the *bana*, and then repeat the *pirit*, or ritual of priestly exorcism."[1] The monks visit the houses of wealthy persons to "say *bana*." Constant attendance on this ceremony or, "hearing *bana*," is made one of the virtues of a Buddhist; and anchorites may leave their retreats to be present when it is read. The priest who officiates wears a yellow robe.

The "nimbus," which is represented as

[1] Wisudhi Margga Sanné, a work written in Pali, by Budhagosha.

surrounding the head of Christ and many of the saints, is of eastern origin. In one of the "Holy Families" by an Italian master, Jesus has three circles about his head, the virgin Mary two; while St. Joseph, John the Baptist, and his mother, have each one circle only. Buddhas is said to have been attended by a nimbus which extended six cubits above his head; while his apostles are represented by native painters as having a similar mark of eminence.

The resemblance between Romanism and Buddhism extends still farther. The Romanist prays thus: —

Heart of Mary, conceived without the stain of sin,
Heart of Mary, full of grace,
Heart of Mary, sanctuary of the Holy Trinity,
Heart of Mary, tabernacle of the Incarnate Word,
Heart of Mary, after God's own heart,
Heart of Mary, illustrious throne of glory,
Heart of Mary, holocaust of divine love,
Heart of Mary, abyss of humility,
Heart of Mary, attached to the cross,
Heart of Mary, seat of mercy,
} *Pray for us.*

The first article in the twenty-first volume

of the Tibetan Do is entitled, "Buddha nama, sahasra pancha, sata chatur, tri panchasat," and is, as the name implies, the enumeration of 5,453 epithets of a Buddha, or Tatagata, each being descriptive of some fancied or real excellence, and are accompanied by a reverential formula; thus, —

I adore the Tatagata, the universally radiant sun;
I adore the Tatagata, the moral wisdom;
I adore the Tatagata, the chief lamp of all the regions of space;

and so on 5,453 lines.[1]

[1] Eastern Monasticism. Spence Hardy.

CHAPTER III.[1]

JEWISH MONKS.

Elijah; John the Baptist. *The Essenes.* Sources from whence their history is drawn; *what* were the Essenes? extracts from Josephus showing them to be a monkish order; *who* were they? Attempts of modern critics to trace their origin. *The Therapeutæ.* Philo's account of them. A theory suggested to account for the origin of these two sects; the Essenes not mentioned in the New Testament; De Quincey identifies them with the early Christians; his theory confuted; attempts made to trace the origin of Christianity to Essenism; who made them; did Jesus Christ belong to this sect; the precepts and practices of each contrasted; this doctrine recently brought to life again; examination of the "Epistles of the Essenes;" the "Swooning" or "Resuscitation" theory, and how it accounts for the resurrection of Jesus; was Jesus Christ a monk?

THE origin of Jewish monasticism is shrouded in uncertainty and doubt. Like the image of Azada in Chaldean history, there comes down to us, from the hoary past

[1] Josephus; Bellum Jud. ii. 8, 2; 13; Antiq. Jud. xiii. 5, 9; xv. 10, 4, 5; xviii. 1, 2–16. Philo Judæus; iii. 523; iv. 219. Wegnern, Victor: Ueber das Verhältniss des Christenthums zum Essenismus (in Zeitschrift für die Historische Theologie, 1841, 2 Heft). For farther reference

of Judaism, the name of a great recluse, the prophet Elijah. He left the abodes of men, and sought the solitude of the wilderness. There is no doubt but that Elijah led a life not materially different from that of the Christian hermits of the first four centuries. He wrestled with the flesh, and received his food from the ravens. St. Benedict and a multitude of Egyptian monks sought a like abode and were fed in the same marvellous manner. An order of Christian monks, the Carmelites, pretend to trace their origin to the prophet Elijah, and have by no means been troubled for arguments to support their claims. They say, that the lives of Elijah and Elias show

consult Der Essäismus und Jesus, von Dr. A. Hilgenfeld, in Zeit. für Wiss. Theol., 1867, 1 Heft. Die Quellen für d. Ges. der Essener, von Dr. W. Clemens, in Zeit. f. Wiss. Theol., 1869, 3 Heft; an essay by De Quincey, The Essennes; Pliny, N. H. v. 17; Joh. Jacob Bellerman, Geschichtnachrichten aus dem Alterthum der Essäer und Therapeuten. Berlin, 1825; Nicol. Serarius de Pharisæis, Saducæis, et Essenis; M. Bernhardi dissertatio de Pharisæis et Essenis; Adolph Roth, Dissertatio de Pharisisæis et Essenis, Jena, 1669; Willemer, de Essenis, Judæorum, Wittenberg, 1680; Joh. Jacob Lange, Dissertatio de Essenis, Halle, 1721.

plainly that they observed the three monastic oaths. God commanded Elijah to secrete himself upon the banks of the brook Cherith, and hence to live in solitude. The children at play called Elias "bald-head," which shows that he wore the tonsure; and his consecration by God with a mantle was the first ceremony of investment in the garb of their order.

Just before the advent of our Saviour there was heard "the voice of one crying in the wilderness;" and we are told that he was "clothed with camel's hair, and with a girdle of skin about his loins; and he did eat locusts and wild honey" (Mark i. 3, 6). It has been suggested by Taylor, the editor of "Calmet's Dictionary of the Bible," that John the Baptist belonged to an order of monks which existed at that time among the Jews, and bore the name of Essenes.

This brings us to the consideration of the first important topic of the present chapter, "What and who were the Essenes?"[1] The

[1] From the Greek word ὅσιος, holy.

sources from which may be drawn the history of this sect are Josephus, Philo, and Pliny; and the order in which these authors are mentioned indicates the respective value of their testimony. Pliny devotes to this subject not more than a dozen lines; Philo, half as many pages; while Josephus gives us a tolerably complete account of the Essenes, their principles, and their mode of life. All three of these accounts agree, with the exception that Pliny says that the members of this sect never married, which is a mistake.

What, then, were the Essenes? They were precisely like the "Dunkers" in Pennsylvania: some of them married, and others did not. They were sometimes assembled in communities, and sometimes they took refuge in the desert. They resembled the "Shakers" of New York and Northern New Hampshire, except that marriage was permitted among them, although it was not recommended. Their principal village or settlement was situated west of the Dead Sea;[1] but Philo informs us that they

[1] See chart, frontispiece.

were to be found in nearly all of the cities and towns of Judæa; and he says that there were more than four thousand of them. The Essenes were a secret society, like the Freemasons; and there were three steps or grades through which each member must pass before all of the secrets of the order were intrusted to him. The length of time occupied by this novitiate was three years. Their organization, principles of action, and mode of life, were in every respect those of a monkish order. They all wore a particular habit, abstained from the use of wine and meat, practised the healing art, prayed much at night, educated the children of strangers, held their goods in common, sank themselves in contemplation, and took the oaths of poverty, obedience, and chastity. It is true that they did not forbid sexual intercourse entirely. There was one order among them of whom Josephus says,—

"They agree with the rest as to their way of living and customs and laws, but differ from them in the point of marriage, as thinking that, by not marrying, they cut off the principal part of human life, which is the prospect of succession; nay, rather that, if all men should be of the same opinion, the whole race of mankind would fail. However, they try their spouses for three months, and if they find that they are every way fitted for the marriage relation, they then marry them. But they do not accompany their wives when they are with child, as an evidence that they do not marry out of regard to pleasure, but for the sake of posterity." (Bellum Jud. II. Chap. 8, 13.)

Philo, on the other hand, referring, without doubt, to the large portion of those who bore this name, writes as follows:—

"They repudiate marriage, and at the same time they practise continence in an eminent degree; for no one of them ever marries a wife, because woman is a selfish creature, and one addicted to jealousy in an immoderate degree, and terribly calculated to agitate and overturn the natural inclinations of man, and to mislead him by her continual tricks; for as she is always studying deceitful speeches and all other kinds of hypocrisy, like an actress on the stage, when she is alluring the eyes and ears of her husband, she proceeds to cajole his predominant mind after the servants have been deceived." (Works, vol. 4, page 221, Bohn's Translation.)

We cannot, perhaps, convey an idea as to the character of this order in any better way than by quoting here a few passages more from Josephus, on whom we mainly rely for our information concerning it.[1]

"They neglect wedlock, but choose out other persons' children while they are pliable, and fit for learning, and esteem them to be of their kindred, and form them according to their own manners. They do not absolutely deny the fitness of marriage and the succession of mankind thereby continued; but they guard against the lascivious behavior of women, and are persuaded that none of them preserve their fidelity to one man."

"These men are despisers of riches, nor is there

[1] Josephus was at heart a great admirer of the Essenes; although he belonged to the sect of the Pharisees, as he informs us in his own life, sec. 2, vol. iv. It is oftentimes stated that he was a member of the Essenian order, which is incorrect, although it is not altogether improbable that he may have served a novitiate among them.

any one to be found among them who hath more than another; for it was a law among them, that those that come to them must let what they have be common to the whole order."

"They are eminent for fidelity, and are the ministers of peace; whatsoever they say also is firmer than an oath; but swearing is avoided by them, and they esteem it worse than perjury.[1] They also take great pains in studying the writings of the ancients; and they inquire after such roots or medicinal stones as may cure their distempers."

"But now, if any one have a mind to come over to their sect, he is not immediately admitted; but he is prescribed the same method of living which they

[1] This practice of the Essenes resembles that recommended by Jesus (Matt. v. 34; xxii. 26). It permitted of exceptions, however, on particularly solemn and important occasions. These very Essenes, who esteemed swearing worse than perjury, compelled a novice, as we are told in the next section, to take tremendous oaths before he was received into full fellowship. The case is the same in Christianity. The apostles, although they agreed with Christ and Saint James (v. 12), in forbidding to swear in general, yet they explain it by "avoiding to swear falsely," and "often and in vain;" and again by "not swearing at all;" but they add, "If that cannot be avoided, swear truly:" all of which sufficiently explains the sense in which their language is to be understood.

use for a year, while he continues excluded: and they give him also a small hatchet, and the forementioned girdle, and the white garment. And when he hath given evidence, during that time, that he can observe their continence, he approaches nearer to their way of living, and is made a partaker of the waters of purification; yet is he not, even now, admitted to live with them; for, after this demonstration of his fortitude, his temper is tried two more years, and if he appear to be worthy, they then admit him into their society. And before he is allowed to touch their common food, he is obliged to take tremendous oaths, that, in the first place, he will exercise piety toward God; and then, that he will observe justice toward men, and that he will do no harm to any one; that he will always hate the wicked and be assistant to the righteous; that he will be perpetually a lover of truth; that he will keep his hand clear from theft, and his soul from unlawful gains; and that he will neither conceal any thing from those of his own sect, nor discover any of their doctrines to others, — no, not though any one should compel him so to do at the hazard of his life. These are the oaths by which they secure their proselytes to themselves."

"Now, after the time of their preparatory trial is over, they are parted into four classes; and so far are the juniors inferior to the seniors, that if the seniors should be touched by the juniors, they must wash themselves, as if they had intermixed themselves with the company of a foreigner."

"These men live the same kind of life as do those whom the Greeks call Pythagoreans."

These quotations will suffice, perhaps, to answer the question, "What were the Essenes?" and we will now proceed to consider "who" they were, and to what circumstances or influences they owed their origin. Here, let it be observed, at the outset, that we tread upon exceedingly difficult ground. After an examination of the most credible opinions upon this subject, the inquirer finds himself straying in a labyrinth of speculations; and his state of mind may be described as something worse than confusion confounded.

Let us mention a few of the theories which have been propounded to account for the origin of this sect:—

1. A class of critics, of whom Bauer and Zeller[1] are the most able representatives, derive Essenism from Greek, or ultimately from Egyptian, sources. According to them, it owed its origin more immediately to the order of Pythagoras, or the mysteries of Orpheus and Bacchus. Quite recently Professor Keim,[2] of the university of Zürich, has come to the support of this theory; and Joseph Langen,[3] a Catholic writer, is also of the same opinion.

2. Dr. A. Hilgenfeld[4] has attempted to trace the origin of this sect to the influence of Buddhism, exerted more immediately through Parseeism, with which the Jews came in contact through their Babylonish branch.

3. Ewald[5] attempts to show that it was

[1] Griech. Philosophie, iii. 2, s. 589, über den Zusammenhang des Essäismus mit dem Griechenthum; Theol. Jahrb. 1856, iii. s. 358.

[2] Der geschichtliche Christus. Zürich, 1865, s. 15.

[3] Das Judenthum in Palästina zur Zeit Christi. Freiburg in Bayern, 1866, s, 186.

[4] Jüdische Apokalyptik. Halle, 1857.

[5] Geschichte des Volks Israel. Bd. iv., s. 476 (Göttingen, 1864).

the natural consequent of Pharisaism; and the Jew Geiger[1] maintains the same opinion.

4. Ritschl[2] thinks that Essenism was the result of the striving after a general priesthood of the children of God. Exodus xix. 6.

We might go on to point out the grounds upon which rests each one of these theories. A remarkable similarity may be discovered between Buddhism, Parseeism, the precepts and practices of Pythagoras, and those laid down in the mysteries of Egypt, on the one hand, and Essenism on the other: but it is only the similarity which exists between a man's appetite and the appetite of his grandfather; and in order to explain the former we do not consult a family genealogy, but rather a work on biology. We set out by maintaining, in our first chapter, that asceticism rested upon a legitimate factor of man's constitution; and human nature may be trusted to repeat itself without the guiding

[1] Das Judenthum und seine Geschichte. Breslau, 1865.

[2] Ueber die Essener; Theol. Jahrb. 1855, s. 315.

influence of a family record. Just as the Spirit of Jesus does not require to be "derived" through an Apostolic Descent, every time it is wanted, but comes to his true disciples whenever two or three are gathered together in his name.

It is true, without doubt, that existing institutions modify the character of those which spring up about them, and give tone in a measure to the public mind; but every social or religious observance rests mainly and ultimately upon human nature, which is the same everywhere and in all ages.

Philo, in his treatise "De Vita Contemplativa," describes an order of ascetics who lived between the Nile and the Red Sea.[1] They bore the name of Therapeutæ (θεράπευται), either, says Philo, because they healed the body, or cured the soul of still more serious maladies. Quite recently a German critic, Hilgenfeld,[2] has attempted to show that they

[1] See chart, frontispiece (3.)

[2] Der Essäismus und Jesus; Zeits. f. Wiss. Theologie, 1867. 1 Band.

owed their name to neither one of these circumstances, but to the fact of their leading a contemplative life. Philo, in describing them, writes thus:—

"They take up their abode outside of walls, or gardens, or solitary lands, seeking for a desert place, not because of any ill-natured misanthropy to which they have learnt to devote themselves, but because of the associations with people of wholly dissimilar dispositions to which they would otherwise be compelled, and which they know to be unprofitable and mischievous."

"And there is the greatest number of such men in Egypt, in every one of the districts, or *nomi* as they are called, and especially around Alexandria." "They do not live near to one another, as men do in cities; for immediate neighborhood to others would be a troublesome and unpleasant thing to men who have conceived an admiration for, and have determined to devote themselves to, solitude; and, on the other hand, they do not live very far from one another, on account of the fellowship which they desire to cultivate, and because of the desirableness of being able to assist one another if they should be attacked by robbers."

Philo, who it is thought was one of their number, often speaks of the Therapeutæ as being the disciples of Moses, — "Their precepts were those of the prophet Moses," &c. This would seem to establish the fact of their being a Jewish sect. The similarity of their observances and mode of life to those of the Essenes would also indicate a common origin and identity with the same. Their chronological and geographical proximity tend to strengthen this conclusion. We have data which enable us to trace the latter as far back as 200, B.C.; while it is probable that their origin was of a much earlier date. If it is thought that the historical development of mankind resembles a chain in which each link clasps the one before it, and is clasped in turn by the one behind; if the history of religions be regarded as a tree the branches of which are supported by a common trunk, — then we would indicate the origin and progress of Jewish asceticism, somewhat as follows:[1] In the chapter on ancient civilization,

[1] See chart, frontispiece.

we have expressed the opinion that the valleys of the Nile and Euphrates were settled by the Cushites or ancient Arabians, at least 7000 B.C. More than four thousand years before the beginning of our era, we read of Azada, a disciple of Saturn, and the founder of asceticism, among the Nabateans. Now these two waves of civilization moved at about the same time, and undoubtedly carried with them nearly the same institutions; hence monkish societies must have been of very ancient origin among the Egyptians, even if we suppose them not to have been of native growth. The children of Israel adopted this institution, as they did many others, from their masters. In crossing the Red Sea, they left the order known by the name of the Therapeutæ, behind them, and just upon the other side. The striking similarity which exists between the Essenes and Therapeutæ cannot perhaps be accounted for in a more satisfactory manner. Any theory of this kind rests, in our opinion, entirely upon supposition: it may however amuse some persons to exercise their inventiveness in this manner.

It is worthy of note that the Essenes are nowhere mentioned in the New Testament. Jesus came in contact with all kinds of people: he conversed with Pharisees, Sadducees, and Samaritans, but never with an Essene. Not even the word is to be found in the Scriptures. Saint Paul, Saint Peter, Saint John, and Saint James utterly overlook them. This silence is still more strange when we consider how nearly the precepts of this sect resembled those taught by Jesus; and it is to be wondered at that no comparison was ever instituted between the two systems. We should naturally expect that Jesus would have commended this sect, but no; not a single word ever fell from his lips concerning them.

This fact will lose some of its singularity when we remember, that the same may be said with regard to the Therapeutæ, who lived, it is true, at a little distance, but, nevertheless, must have been well known, and were without doubt a Jewish sect.

Even the Sadducees are mentioned but once or twice; and the carelessness of a monkish transcriber might have deprived us of even that. As for any friendly mention of the Essenes by Jesus, we should not be led to expect it from his treatment of the Pharisees, whom he denounced in the severest manner, although he chose from among their number the most of his disciples. So that this resemblance between the teachings of Jesus and those of the Essenes, instead of rendering his failure to commend them more remarkable, would help to explain it.

De Quincey[1] maintains the identity of the Essenes and the early Christians. He denies emphatically that any such sect ever existed among the Jews; but his intemperate and indecent denunciation of Josephus, taken together with the not altogether scholarly argument, that Essenism should not be al-

1 The Essenes, in his His. and Crit. Essays, vol. i.

lowed to antedate Christianity, lest it should rob the latter of the originality of its moral teachings, shake somewhat our confidence in his ability as a biblical critic. In this very article, he quotes Josephus, who says, "the Essenes put up prayers which they *received from their forefathers.*" Now Josephus was born about five years after the crucifixion of Jesus: how then could he speak of the observances of a Christian sect as though they had come down from the hoary past? How will De Quincey dispose of the moral doctrines of the Therapeutæ, which resembled so nearly those of the Essenes, and which Philo, who was a contemporary of Josephus, tells us were handed down to them from the prophet Moses?

We may discuss here the relation which Christianity bore to Essenism, and take into consideration the probability of the one having given birth to the other. It has generally been thought that Voltaire[1] and Frederick the

[1] Compare his Dictionnaire Philosophique; Art. Esséniens.

Great,[1] were the first to trace the origin of Christianity to the Essenian order. This, however, is a mistake. Voltaire resided for a time in England, and became acquainted with English thought, to which he was indebted for much of his philosophy. Bolingbroke, often quoted by Voltaire, indicates Essenism as the origin of Christianity; and Prideaux[2] declares that such was the belief of the deists in his time. A German writer, Johann Georg Wachter, advanced the same opinion as early as 1713.[3] In modern times,

[1] Frederick the Great, in a letter addressed to D'Alembert (18th Oct. 1770), writes as follows: "Permit me to say that our present Christianity resembles the religion of Christ about as much as it does that of the Iroquois. Jesus was a Jew, and we burn the Jews; Jesus taught forbearance, and we persecute; Jesus advocated a good system of morals, and we do not practise it; Jesus never established a dogma, and the councils have provided richly for them. In short, a Christian of the third century resembles in nothing one of the first. *Jesus was properly an Essene; he adopted the moral system of the Essenes, which differs but little from that of Zeno.*" Œuvres, Berlin, t. xi. p. 94.

[2] The Old and New Testament in connection with the History of the Jews, &c.

[3] This work exists only in manuscript, and bears the title, De Primordiis Christianæ Religionis Libri Duo, &c. It may be seen in the library of the University of Wittenberg.

Stäudlin[1] has been, without doubt, the most able defender of this doctrine. Reim[2] has also called attention to the fact that Epiphanius[3] says that the Christians were merely successors of the Essenes. The Freemasons in Germany[4] were among the first to take up this theory, and they entered zealously upon its defence; since they had long maintained their descent from the Essenes; and they hoped to increase their dignity by proving the common origin of their order and Christianity.

Stäudlin expresses the opinion that it is very probable that Jesus, while yet a boy, became an inmate of one of the schools of the Essenes, and was educated and prepared by them, with the express intention of sending

1 Geschichte der Sittenlehre Jesu. Göttingen, 1799, s. 570.

2 Christus und die Vernunft, s. 685.

3 Lib. i. Haeres x., xxix.

4 Compare Ragotzky, der Freidenker in der Maurerei. Berlin, 1793, s. 183–192. Lenning, Encyklopädie der Freimaurerei, 2 b. art. Essener. On the other hand, Fichte and Mörlin have declared themselves opposed to this view.

him into the world, later in life, for the purpose of bringing about a great moral revolution. We have already quoted a passage from Josephus in which he says that the Essenes took other people's children to educate them. By others, it has been supposed that Jesus passed the eighteen years which intervened between his appearance in the temple at Jerusalem, and the opening of his ministry, in Egypt, where he fitted himself for his work. Each one must decide for himself how much weight ought to be attached to such speculations. There is no doubt that Jesus was educated very much above the masses, else he could not have read and expounded the law in the synagogues. It is not at all probable, however, that he ever was a member of the order of Essenes or of that of the Therapeutae. The members of these sects were bound by heavy oaths not to reveal their doctrines, while Jesus bade his disciples declare their truth upon the housetops. If Stäudlin's theory is correct, why were not his disciples furnished him out of the order which had taken so much pains to prepare him for his work. The widest difference existed between the precepts of Jesus and those of the Essenes, even when they seemed to resemble each other the most. Both advised celibacy, but for altogether different reasons. The latter were opposed to marriage on dualistic grounds; they believed all of the propensities of the body to be absolutely bad, and the work of an evil spirit.[1] Jesus did not oppose the institution in itself, but advised celibacy in order that his disciples might be left free to advance his kingdom. Saint Paul was of the same opinion, for a like reason. The troubled and agitated state of society, together with the constant expectation of the speedy reappearance of the Messiah to judge the world, made the single state seem preferable to marriage. The severe fasting of the Essenes stands in open contrast with the practice of Jesus; and when the dis-

[1] This statement may seem to conflict with a passage already quoted from Philo, but a careful examination of the subject will justify us, I think, in the above assertion.

ciples of John the Baptist and the Pharisees reproached him with his mode of life (Matt. ix. 14; Mark ii. 18; Luke v. 33), he replied to them, "Can the children of the bride chamber mourn, as long as the bridegroom is with them?" Moreover, if Christ had prescribed regular fasts, it is more likely that he imitated in this the law of Moses, rather than that of the Essenes. Finally, for the points of difference are almost innumerable, we may regard as decisive the single statement of Josephus, who says, that if a senior was touched by a junior "he must wash himself as if he had intermixed himself with the company of a foreigner." This single ordinance stamps the order as strictly Jewish. How will such a practice, however, compare with the precept of Jesus, who taught that "the first should be last and the last first;" and who himself insisted upon washing the feet of his disciples. The long interval between the twelfth and thirtieth years of Jesus, and concerning which the New Testament preserves an absolute silence, may leave room for the exercise of inventive genius; but no one need wonder at the silence of the sacred writers with regard to this portion of our Saviour's life, for it should be remembered that the four Gospels are in no wise meant to be a biography of Jesus. Their purpose is simply to present to our view the Messiah, the Christ.

This theory, which makes Christianity an outgrowth of Essenism, although permitted to slumber for a time, has recently been seized upon again by German sceptics, whose position grew more and more uncomfortable as the impression gained ground that the historical evidences upon which the miracles and resurrection of Jesus Christ are known to rest, have resisted the severest test of criticism to which it was possible for them to be put. Strauss himself declares that of these two suppositions, — first, either Jesus died, and in that case was not seen afterwards; or else, second, he did not die, and subsequently appeared to his disciples: he judges the latter to be the most probable conclusion. Soon after this concession was made, the "Resuscitationists" (ground between the two millstones of a low naturalism, and the overwhelming evidence which has been brought to show that many persons died in the belief that they had seen Jesus after his crucifixion) came forward with their theory. It was by no means an altogether new one. About the beginning of the present century, Venturini and Bahrdt advanced the same views. The former published an infamous work at Copenhagen, in 1800, with the following title, "Natürliche Geschichte des grossen Propheten von Nazareth."

In addition to this, a new forgery has been put upon the world in the form of a series of letters, which it is pretended were found in a monastery, and purport to have been written by a member of the Essenian order. We learn from this source, that Jesus was a member of that order, was versed in their methods of healing, and filled with their spirit. They watched his course with great interest, and interceded through Pilate for his release. This attempt having proved abortive, on account of the hate of the Jewish people, who refused to release him, they resorted to a trick by which Jesus (some of his guards being in the interest of the Essenes, who exerted a secret influence in society like that of the Freemasons of to-day) was cut down before life became extinct, and conveyed to one of the monasteries of his order, where he was resuscitated, and, after having ventured out a single time in order that he might see his disciples, returned thither, and passed there in seclusion the remainder of his days. The welcome given to Jesus wherever he went, the frequent visits of eager and curious friends, are both to be explained by supposing that his hosts and guests were members of his own fraternity. The three wise men of the East were probably Essenian elders who came to visit the child, and secure it, if possible, that it might be educated in one of the monasteries of their order.

It is truly encouraging when the self-styled friends of reason and progress are forced to resort to such puerile measures, in order to make front against those whom they are accustomed to denounce as bigoted and superstitious. For the consolation of this latter class, we will give a few quotations from these "Epistles of the Essenes," which lie at the foundation of this doctrine of "Resuscitation," which has found its defenders not only in Europe, but in the theological schools of America, and still finds expression, now and then, through some of our religious and philosophical journals: —

"You have blamed us, my dear brethren, because we failed to rescue our friend from crucifixion by means of our secret agencies. But I do not need to remind you, that, in the first place, our rule forbids us to act openly, — and in this law may be found the explanation why Jesus never alludes in the Scriptures to his connection with the Essenian Order, — and, in the second place, we had two capable and experienced members of our fraternity zealously employed, one in the council of the Jews, and the other near Pilate, but their efforts were in vain, since Jesus himself desired to die in the cause of truth and virtue, and in order that the measure of the law might be fulfilled."

We are informed that Jesus, after seven hours, weakened by the maltreatment which he had suffered previous to the execution, and overpowered by the influence of the oppressive atmosphere (which in that region was frequently disturbed by violent storms accompanied by earthquakes), fell into a state of unconsciousness. A rigidness of the body, even so as to present every appearance of death, is, we are told, under such circumstances, a supposition so natural and so consistent with physiological principles, that one can scarcely comprehend that credulous fanaticism which rises up with such scornful rage and unyielding obstinacy against this extremely probable assumption.

"Towards evening a few of the Essenian Brotherhood came to the place of execution, and were immediately impressed with the possibility of a rescue. Joseph and Nicodemus examined the body, and then the latter drew Joseph hurriedly to one side and said,—'As true as I am initiated in the knowledge of the body and the phenomena of life, so sure is a rescue possible.' One of the persons present, who was not a member of the order, was sent off to the city on what might be called a fool's-errand, while the body was being taken down. Not far from the place of execution, there was a cloister belonging to their order from whence restoratives were quickly brought, and whither Jesus was conveyed after his return to consciousness. Thus the angels of the gospel record transform themselves into the hospitable brothers of this monastery, whose white garments were well calculated, especially when taken together with the terror of an earthquake, to frighten the timid and superstitious guards, and the next day to fill the minds of the women, already excited by grief and love, with extraordinary alarm. Jesus subsequently met his disciples in a quiet spot near his retreat. He exhorted them to be brave and abounding in faith. The longer he spoke, the more impressive grew the tones of his voice; and at last he seemed like one inspired. He prayed for his friends whom he must now abandon, and lifting his hand he blessed them. As he did this, a cloud or a volume of fog swept over the top of the mountain, already touched and gilded by the setting sun, and hid him from their view. Two of the brethren now come to him to say it was late; and, while his disciples were yet bowed upon the earth, Jesus departed."

He was induced to take this step by the following argument, —

"Retire into the midst of the devoted men who revere you. The people, who do not understand your teachings, are debating how you may be made a temporal ruler, and the Roman yoke thereby shaken off. But it is no part of your plan to attempt the advancement of the 'Kingdom of Heaven' by war and revolution. Therefore retire into the solitude; pass the remainder of your days in privacy, surrounded by your Essenian brethren; and rest assured that thy word will not die in thy disciples."

How insignificant seem the aberrations of the human intellect when confronted with this discovery; how few the steps towards unprejudiced thought and inquiry which have been made since the days of the crucifixion; how small and puerile seem the petty contentions of the priestly opposition against *rational progress;* how selfish, when compared with its beneficent results to the human race! Truly the fruit of human knowledge seems destined to move only in periods of a thousand years each.

It remains for us to consider, in conclusion, this question, "Was Jesus Christ a monk?" It has already been made sufficiently clear, we think, that he belonged to no existing order or sect of this character; but Christian ascetics in all ages have sought to find the warrant for their own mode of life in that of their Master. It is easy enough to discover passages in the New Testament which, by themselves, would seem to favor a contemplative life. There are two methods, however, of quoting Scripture,— one is to select isolated texts, and in this way one may prove any thing he chooses to undertake; and the other method is to consider the general tone and spirit of the sacred writings.

"What is happiness?" demands an eastern ascetic. "A lamp sheltered from the wind." The Christianity of Jesus Christ was a combat with the world, a struggle against selfishness and pride. "Instead of attempting to reform the world, like Buddha, by the establishment of monastic institutions, he preached a morality accessible to all, — a morality which was good for the master and good for the slave, for the virgin and for the soldier, for every heart capable of understanding the Scriptures and disposed to love them. To despair of seeing the precepts of the gospel dominant upon the earth; to fly in disgust to the solitude of a desert, in order to escape the orgies of a society fallen into decay; to think solely of saving one's own soul without concern for the salvation of our fellow-men, — is this to act as true disciples of him who passed all of his life surrounded by publicans and sinners? Is it to imitate the disciples, who — alone in the world, ignorant and feeble—dared to attack, at the same time, Judaism and idolatry? Suppose these fishermen had despaired of converting the world, and, shaking off from their feet the dust of Jerusalem, of Athens, of Corinth, and of Rome, had gone to weep in the desert and bemoan the irremediable corruption of the world! To despair of the cause of virtue and of truth, is this to place complete confidence in the power and in the goodness of our heavenly Father?"

The spirit of monasticism is selfishness: it is the avoidance of all moral responsibility, and results in spiritual apathy. We have seen the Fakirs of India attain to a degree of immobility almost complete. While the West has sought so often, says one, after the "perpetual motion," the East still struggles to find the "absolute repose." The entire ministry of our Saviour was devoted to action; but if the theory of monasticism is correct, then Simon the Stylite, who passed many years perched upon the top of a column, attained to a greater degree of perfection than did the Son of God. Jesus participated in the marriage feast at Cana, ate frequently at the table of his friends, and was accused on this account of being "a glutton and a wine-bibber." Instead of taking up his residence upon the gloomy shores of the Red Sea, he fixed his abode at Capernaum, upon the beautiful banks of the lake of Genesareth. "Ye who disfigure in yourselves the work of God, how dare you recognize him as the messenger of heaven?"

The subject of celibacy we have already considered in another place, and pointed out the difference between the Scripture doctrine on this subject and that of monasticism.

The poverty and humility of the monks have oftentimes been quoted as points of resemblance between them and our Divine Master, but the Old World has long since become used to the anomaly of seeing those who pretend to despise the goods of this earth in possession of the best part of the wealth of those countries where they are permitted to exist. They have also been made to understand how a man may be individually poor, and yet possessed of immense riches in company with others. The scandalous wealth of the monasteries has long been well known. A monk, too, when taken alone, is supposed to be humble; but, when taken with the great church to which he belongs, his arrogance knows no bounds. He may often be heard to utter, with the Franciscan monk Ximenes, these blasphemous words: " Never forget that I hold your queen every day at my feet, and your God in my hands."

Humility is the garb with which God clothes the pious soul: pride is the devil's livery.

Cambridge: Stereotyped and Printed by John Wilson and Son.

www.ingramcontent.com/pod-product-compliance
Lightning Source LLC
LaVergne TN
LVHW021404110826
845150LV00007B/1779

* 9 7 8 1 4 2 5 5 1 2 7 6 7 *